When Quiet Meets Loud

The Complete Guide to Thriving with ADHD and Borderline Personality Disorder Together

Leyla Maro Walter

Copyright © 2024 by Leyla Maro Walter. All rights reserved.

First Edition 2024

ISBN: 978-1-923604-74-2

This book is for informational and educational purposes only and is not intended as a substitute for professional medical advice, diagnosis, or treatment. Always seek the advice of your physician, psychiatrist, therapist, or other qualified health provider with any questions you may have regarding medical or mental health conditions. Never disregard professional medical advice or delay in seeking it because of something you have read in this book.

The author shares insights based on research and lived experience. The strategies and suggestions presented are not suitable for everyone and should be discussed with qualified healthcare providers before implementation.

Any discussion of medications in this book is for educational purposes only. Medication decisions should only be made in consultation with qualified medical professionals who know your complete medical history.

If you are experiencing a mental health crisis, having thoughts of self-harm or suicide, please contact emergency services (911 in the US) or crisis support:

- National Suicide Prevention Lifeline: 988
- Crisis Text Line: Text HOME to 741741

All names and identifying details of individuals mentioned in this book have been changed to protect privacy. Any resemblance to actual persons, living or dead, or actual events is purely coincidental. Case examples are composites drawn from multiple sources and do not represent any single individual.

Individual results from applying the concepts in this book will vary. Recovery and management of ADHD and BPD are highly individual processes that depend on many factors including but not limited to severity of symptoms, access to treatment, support systems, and co-occurring conditions.

Table of Contents

Preface 1

Section I: Understanding the Storm Within 4

    Chapter 1: When Quiet Meets Loud 5

    Chapter 2: The Tangled Brain 15

    Chapter 3: Diagnostic Confusion 26

    Chapter 4: The Identity Puzzle 38

Section II: Treatment That Actually Works 49

    Chapter 5: DBT Meets ADHD 50

    Chapter 6: Medication Matters - Stimulants, Safety, and Stability 63

    Chapter 7: Beyond DBT - CBT, Schema Therapy, and Integrated Approaches 75

    Chapter 8: Crisis Planning When You Have Two Ticking Clocks 86

Section III: Daily Life Strategies 96

    Chapter 9: Relationships - When Attachment Meets Attention ... 97

    Chapter 10: Emotional Storms and Executive Function 108

    Chapter 11: Work, Career, and Finding Your Place 118

    Chapter 12: The Body Connection 129

Section IV: Building Your Life 140

    Chapter 13: Family Healing and Support Systems 141

    Chapter 14: Trauma, Resilience, and Post-Traumatic Growth .. 155

    Chapter 15: Life Transitions and Major Decisions 165

    Chapter 16: Recovery Is Real - Long-Term Success with BPD-ADHD 175

Appendices **186**
   Appendix A: Quick Reference Guides...187
   Appendix B: Resources for Families and Clinicians 198
   Appendix C: Worksheets and Tools 204

Reference..**210**

Preface

This book was born from frustration – my own and that of countless others who've been told their struggles don't quite fit the diagnostic manual. For years, mental health professionals have treated ADHD and Borderline Personality Disorder as separate entities, forcing people to choose which label fits best. But for the 30-60% of people with BPD who also have ADHD, this either/or approach has been disastrous.

When I set out to write this book, I knew it couldn't follow traditional mental health book formats. Why? Because traditional formats assume neurotypical processing – the ability to maintain focus through lengthy theoretical discussions, remember complex concepts and process information linearly. If you have ADHD and BPD, your brain doesn't work that way. Neither does mine.

How This Book Is Different

Each chapter follows a specific structure designed for brains that need multiple entry points and processing styles:

Every chapter begins with a real (though anonymized) story. Not because stories are entertaining, but because ADHD brains often process narrative better than abstract concepts, and BPD brains need emotional connection to engage. These aren't random anecdotes – they're carefully chosen to illustrate the exact intersection of symptoms you're about to explore.

Information is broken into digestible sections with descriptive headers. Your ADHD brain can jump to what's relevant right now. Your BPD brain can find what matches your current emotional state. No long walls of text that trigger dissociation or overwhelm.

This isn't academic writing. It's me talking to you, human to human, about things that are hard. The language is deliberately simple – not because you're not smart (you probably are), but because complex syntax is harder to process when you're dysregulated or distracted.

I use "you" throughout. Some might find this presumptuous, but I chose it because connection matters for BPD brains, and direct address maintains ADHD attention better than abstract third-person discussions.

Sometimes I'm irreverent about our struggles. Not to minimize them, but because laughing at the absurdity can be healing. If that doesn't work for you, skip those parts.

Key concepts appear multiple times in different contexts. This isn't poor editing – it's designed redundancy for when you can't remember what you read yesterday or when emotional states make different explanations resonate.

I won't tell you everything happens for a reason or that you're special because of your conditions. Some days, having ADHD and BPD just sucks. This book acknowledges that reality while still offering genuine hope based on research and lived experience.

How to Use This Book

You don't have to read it cover to cover. In fact, you probably won't – and that's fine. Here are different ways to approach it:

Crisis Mode: Go straight to Chapter 8 (Crisis Planning) and Appendix A (Quick Reference Guides).

Newly Diagnosed: Start with Part I to understand what's happening in your brain.

Been in Treatment for Years: Jump to Part II for adapted strategies you might not have tried.

Supporting Someone: Read Chapter 13 (Family Healing) first, then Part I for understanding.

Professional Seeking Resources: Appendix B has clinical tools and treatment planning guides.

Read it in whatever order makes sense for your current state. Skip chapters that don't apply. Return to sections when you need them. This book is a tool, not a test.

A Note About Hope

Throughout this book, I talk about recovery. Let me be clear: recovery doesn't mean cure. You will likely always have ADHD and BPD traits. Recovery means learning to work with your brain instead of against it, building a life that accommodates your neurodivergence, and finding meaning despite – or because of – your differences.

The research is clear: 50-70% of people with BPD achieve significant symptom remission. ADHD can be effectively managed with the right supports. When both are treated together, outcomes improve dramatically. These aren't inspirational platitudes – they're statistics from longitudinal studies.

The path isn't straight. Progress isn't linear. But recovery is real, and it's waiting for you.

Leyla Maro Walter

Section I: Understanding the Storm Within
Foundations of BPD-ADHD Comorbidity

Chapter 1: When Quiet Meets Loud

Sarah sat in her therapist's office for what felt like the hundredth time, though it was really only her seventh visit with this new provider. At 34, she'd been through the mental health system enough times to lose count. Depression at 16. Anxiety at 20. Bipolar disorder at 23 (later rescinded). Borderline personality disorder at 28. But something still wasn't right.

"I feel like I'm drowning in my own thoughts," she said, her leg bouncing rapidly under the table. "Everyone says I'm 'too dramatic,' but they don't understand – my brain never stops. I can't finish anything. I start a project with all this passion, then I hate myself for abandoning it. I know the DBT skills, but when I try to use them, my mind is already ten steps ahead, catastrophizing about something else entirely."

Her therapist leaned forward slightly. "Sarah, has anyone ever evaluated you for ADHD?"

The question hung in the air. ADHD? But she wasn't hyperactive like those kids in school who couldn't sit still. She was the emotional one, the intense one, the one whose moods swung like a pendulum. Sure, she fidgeted and lost things constantly, but wasn't that just her being scattered from all the emotional chaos?

Two months and a comprehensive evaluation later, Sarah finally had her answer: ADHD, combined type, co-occurring with borderline personality disorder. For the first time in her adult life, the full picture made sense.

The Hidden Epidemic Nobody's Talking About

Here's something that might blow your mind: between 30 and 60 percent of people diagnosed with borderline personality disorder also have ADHD. Read that again. **Up to 60 percent**. We're talking about millions of people walking around with both conditions, most of them undiagnosed or misdiagnosed for years, sometimes decades.

Why isn't anyone talking about this? Well, for starters, the mental health field has a bad habit of putting conditions in neat little boxes. You're either this or that. You have a personality disorder or a neurodevelopmental condition. You're emotional or you're scattered. But human brains? They don't care about our diagnostic categories.

The research on this overlap is relatively new, and frankly, it's turning everything we thought we knew on its head. Studies from major psychiatric centers are showing that not only do these conditions frequently co-occur, but when they do, they create a unique symptom profile that's more than just the sum of its parts.

Think about it this way: BPD affects roughly 1.6 percent of the adult population. ADHD affects about 4.4 percent. But here's where the math gets interesting – if you have one of these conditions, your chances of having the other skyrocket. It's not random coincidence. There's something deeper going on.

Why These Conditions Love to Travel Together

So what's behind this massive overlap? Buckle – sorry, *prepare yourself* for some fascinating science that actually makes sense.

First up: genetics. Recent twin studies have found a whopping **72 percent genetic correlation** between BPD and ADHD. That's huge. To put it in perspective, that's a stronger genetic link than between depression and anxiety, conditions everyone assumes go hand in hand. Your genes don't determine your destiny, but they do load the gun, so to speak.

These shared genes affect some pretty important stuff:

- How your brain produces and uses dopamine (your motivation and reward chemical)
- How your emotional regulation systems develop
- How your executive function networks wire themselves
- How sensitive you are to rejection and criticism
- How your brain processes stress and trauma

But genes are just part of the story. Environment matters too, and here's where things get really interesting. Both conditions are associated with similar early life experiences:

Childhood trauma or neglect affects about 70 percent of people with BPD and 45 percent of people with ADHD. Not everyone with these conditions has trauma, but the overlap is significant.

Invalidating environments – places where your emotions or struggles aren't recognized or are actively dismissed – are huge risk factors for both conditions. Think about a kid with undiagnosed ADHD constantly being told they're lazy or not trying hard enough. Now add emotional sensitivity to the mix. That's a perfect storm for developing both conditions.

Early attachment disruptions play a role too. When a child's needs aren't consistently met – maybe because a parent is struggling with their own mental health, or there's chaos in the home – it affects how the brain develops emotional regulation and attention systems.

The Loud and Quiet Dance

Here's something crucial to understand: BPD symptoms tend to be **louder** than ADHD symptoms. They demand attention. The emotional storms, the relationship crises, the self-harm behaviors – these are what bring people to treatment. Meanwhile, ADHD symptoms often hide in the background, mistaken for personality quirks or blamed on the emotional chaos.

Let me paint you a picture of how this plays out:

You're in a relationship argument. Your BPD is screaming about abandonment, making you feel like you're going to die if this person leaves. But underneath that, your ADHD is making it impossible to track the conversation. You can't remember what was said five minutes ago. You interrupt because if you don't say your thought right now, it'll disappear. You're simultaneously overwhelmed by emotion AND unable to organize your thoughts enough to express them clearly.

Or take work situations. Everyone sees when you have an emotional reaction to criticism – that's the loud BPD part. What they don't see is that you missed half the instructions because you were distracted, or that you've been masking your confusion for years because you're terrified of being seen as incompetent.

The ADHD symptoms become like background noise you've gotten so used to that you don't even recognize them as symptoms anymore. They're just "how you are":

- Always losing things? "I'm just disorganized."
- Can't finish projects? "I'm a failure."
- Constantly late? "I'm inconsiderate."
- Mind racing? "I overthink everything."

The Gender Factor That Changes Everything

Women face a particularly rough road when it comes to getting accurately diagnosed with both conditions. ADHD in women is already underdiagnosed because it often presents as inattentiveness rather than hyperactivity. Add BPD to the mix, and the diagnostic picture gets even murkier.

Young girls with ADHD often develop incredible masking skills. They learn to hide their struggles, to appear "normal," to compensate through anxiety and perfectionism. By the time they hit adolescence or young adulthood, those coping mechanisms start breaking down. Enter: what looks like BPD.

But here's the thing – sometimes it IS BPD. Sometimes it's ADHD that's been misdiagnosed as BPD. And sometimes, more often than we realized, it's both.

Women with both conditions often report:

- Being called "too sensitive" their whole lives
- Feeling like they're constantly performing "normal"
- Exhaustion from trying to keep it all together
- Intense shame about their struggles with "simple" tasks
- Being labeled as dramatic when they're actually overwhelmed

The hormonal component adds another layer. ADHD symptoms often worsen during PMS, pregnancy, and menopause. BPD symptoms can fluctuate with hormones too. Put them together, and you've got a monthly (or daily) rollercoaster that no one seems to understand, least of all the woman experiencing it.

Cultural Considerations Most Doctors Miss

Culture shapes how we experience and express both ADHD and BPD symptoms, but most diagnostic tools and treatments were developed studying white, middle-class populations. This creates huge barriers for people from different cultural backgrounds.

In some cultures, emotional expression is encouraged and seen as normal. What might be labeled as "emotional dysregulation" in one context could be completely acceptable in another. Conversely, cultures that highly value emotional restraint might lead to delayed diagnosis because people have learned to hide their struggles too well.

ADHD symptoms also get interpreted differently across cultures. In communities where extended family is heavily involved in child-rearing, a child's attention difficulties might be compensated for by the village-style support. It's only when they leave that environment that the struggles become apparent.

For people of color, there's an added layer: the very real fear of being stereotyped or pathologized. Black women with emotional intensity might be labeled "angry" rather than recognized as struggling with BPD. Latino men might have their ADHD hyperactivity dismissed as machismo. Asian individuals might have both conditions overlooked entirely due to model minority myths.

Immigration and intergenerational trauma add complexity too. When your family has survived war, displacement, or systemic oppression, distinguishing between trauma responses, cultural adaptation, and neurodevelopmental conditions becomes incredibly complex.

The Frontolimbic Network: Where It All Goes Down

Now for the brain science, but don't worry – I'll keep it real and relevant to your daily life.

Both ADHD and BPD involve disruptions in something called the frontolimbic network. Think of this as the communication highway between your emotional centers (limbic system) and your thinking, planning, decision-making centers (frontal lobe). When this highway has traffic jams, construction zones, and detours, you get the symptoms of both conditions.

In ADHD, the frontal lobe (particularly the prefrontal cortex) is underactive. It's like having a sleepy traffic controller who can't keep the cars moving efficiently. This affects:

- Focus and attention
- Planning and organization
- Impulse control
- Working memory
- Time awareness

In BPD, the limbic system (especially the amygdala) is overactive, like having emergency vehicles with sirens blaring constantly trying to get through. This affects:

- Emotional intensity
- Threat detection
- Fear responses
- Attachment feelings
- Stress reactions

When you have both conditions, it's like having a sleepy traffic controller trying to manage constant emergency vehicles. The emotional signals are too strong, and the regulatory systems are too weak. No wonder everything feels chaotic.

Your Personal Assessment Checklist

Let's get practical. Here's a checklist to help you identify how both conditions might be showing up in your life. This isn't a diagnostic tool – only a qualified professional can diagnose you – but it can help you organize your thoughts for that conversation.

ADHD Signs Often Hidden by BPD:

- You've always lost things, even before the emotional problems started
- Your room/house goes through cycles of chaos and frantic organizing
- You have 47 unfinished projects that you started with passion
- Reading is hard unless you're completely obsessed with the topic
- You interrupt people not to be rude, but because thoughts evaporate
- Sitting through movies is torture unless you're doing something else

- You're either laser-focused or can't focus at all – no middle ground
- Time blindness has ruined more relationships than you can count

BPD Signs That Might Be Intensified by ADHD:

- Your emotional reactions feel too fast to catch
- Impulsive behaviors happen before you even realize you're upset
- Identity confusion is worse because you can't stick with anything
- Relationship patterns are chaotic partly because you forget the good times
- Self-harm urges spike when you're overwhelmed by tasks
- Abandonment fears get triggered by ADHD-related mistakes
- Emptiness feels worse when you can't complete meaningful activities
- Anger explodes when executive dysfunction meets emotional pain

The Overlap Zone:

- Rejection sensitive dysphoria that feels like death
- Substance use to calm both the chaos and the pain
- Chronic feelings of failure and defectiveness
- Social difficulties that stem from both conditions
- Sleep problems that make everything worse
- Sensory sensitivities that trigger emotional storms

- Perfectionism alternating with complete giving up
- Feeling like an alien trying to pass as human

Making Sense of Your Story

Understanding that you have both conditions isn't about collecting labels or making excuses. It's about finally having a map that matches the territory of your actual life. For years, you've probably been trying to navigate with incomplete or wrong maps, beating yourself up for getting lost.

Maybe you've been in DBT groups where everyone else seemed to "get it" faster than you. That might be your ADHD making it harder to absorb the skills. Maybe you've tried ADHD strategies that fell apart the moment you had an emotional crisis. That's the BPD throwing a wrench in the works.

Or maybe, like Sarah, you've been told you're "too much" your whole life. Too emotional. Too scattered. Too intense. Too inconsistent. Too everything. But here's the truth: you're not too much. **You have two neurobiological conditions that affect how your brain works**. That's not a character flaw or a personal failing. It's just neurology.

Moving Forward With Both

So where does this leave you? Actually, in a better place than you might think. Understanding both conditions means you can:

- Stop blaming yourself for struggles that have neurobiological roots
- Get treatment that addresses both conditions
- Understand why some strategies haven't worked
- Develop self-compassion for your unique challenges
- Connect with others who share your dual diagnosis
- Advocate for your needs more effectively

The path forward isn't about choosing which condition to focus on or pretending one doesn't exist. It's about understanding how they interact in YOUR specific brain and life, and building strategies that work for your unique neurology.

What This Means for Your Life

Having both BPD and ADHD isn't a life sentence to chaos and suffering. Yes, it's challenging. Yes, it requires more complex treatment. Yes, you'll need to work harder than neurotypical people to manage daily life. But you're also capable of incredible creativity, deep empathy, passionate engagement with life, and unique insights that come from experiencing the world differently.

The key is to stop trying to force yourself into neurotypical boxes and start building a life that works with your brain, not against it. That starts with understanding what you're working with – which is exactly what we'll explore in the next chapters.

Chapter 2: The Tangled Brain

Picture your brain for a moment. Not the pink, wrinkled thing from anatomy class, but the living, electric, constantly changing command center that makes you who you are. Now imagine trying to run incredibly complex software – your thoughts, emotions, behaviors – on hardware that's wired a bit differently than the standard model. That's what we're dealing with when we talk about ADHD and BPD.

But here's what nobody tells you: different doesn't mean broken. Your brain isn't malfunctioning; it's functioning according to a different blueprint. Understanding that blueprint – really understanding it, not just intellectually but in a way that makes sense of your daily experience – that's where real change begins.

What Brain Scans Reveal About Your Daily Struggles

When researchers put people with ADHD and BPD in brain scanners, they don't just see random differences. They see specific, consistent patterns that explain so much about why life feels the way it does.

Let's start with what happens when you're just lying there, doing nothing. Even at rest, your brain looks different. In ADHD, certain areas – especially in the frontal lobe – show less activity. It's like they're running on power-saving mode. In BPD, emotional areas are hyperactive, like they're constantly scanning for threats even when you're trying to relax.

But here's where it gets really interesting: when you have both conditions, these patterns don't just add up – they interact. The underactive frontal regions can't properly regulate the overactive emotional regions. It's like having a guard dog that barks at everything while the person who's supposed to train it is taking a nap.

During emotional tasks – say, looking at faces with different expressions – the BPD brain lights up like a Christmas tree, especially in the amygdala (your alarm system). The ADHD brain shows delayed or weak responses in areas that should help interpret and regulate those alarms. Together? You get intense emotional reactions that your brain can't efficiently process or control.

When doing focus tasks, the ADHD brain struggles to maintain consistent activation in attention networks. Add BPD to the mix, and emotional areas keep interrupting, like someone constantly changing the channel while you're trying to watch a show.

Dopamine: The Chemical Everyone's Talking About

You've probably heard about dopamine, especially if you've researched ADHD. But there's more to this story than "ADHD means low dopamine." Both conditions involve dopamine disruptions, but in fascinatingly different ways.

Dopamine isn't just about pleasure or reward – it's about motivation, future planning, and something called "salience" (basically, what your brain decides is important enough to pay attention to). In ADHD, the dopamine system is inefficient. You might have:

- Fewer dopamine receptors
- Dopamine that gets cleared away too quickly
- Problems with dopamine release

This is why stimulant medications work – they help dopamine stick around longer and work better.

But BPD also involves dopamine issues, particularly in how it relates to attachment and social reward. Your brain might overreact to social rewards (like approval) and under-react to non-social rewards (like completing tasks). This creates a perfect storm: you desperately need social validation but can't consistently do the things that would earn it.

The intersection is brutal. Your ADHD brain needs more stimulation to feel normal, so you might seek intense experiences. Your BPD brain interprets these intense experiences through an attachment lens, creating unstable relationships and identity confusion. Meanwhile, both conditions make it hard to learn from consequences because the reward system isn't calibrating properly.

Executive Function Meets Emotional Dysregulation

Executive function is your brain's CEO – it plans, organizes, makes decisions, and controls impulses. Emotional regulation is your brain's HR department – it manages feelings, maintains stability, and helps you respond appropriately to situations. When both departments are struggling, the whole company falls apart.

In ADHD, executive function problems are the core issue. You might struggle with:

- **Working memory** (holding information in mind while using it)
- **Cognitive flexibility** (switching between tasks or adapting to changes)
- **Inhibitory control** (stopping yourself from doing or saying something)

In BPD, emotional dysregulation is center stage. You might experience:

- **Emotional sensitivity** (feeling things faster and more intensely)
- **Emotional reactivity** (bigger responses to emotional triggers)
- **Slow return to baseline** (taking longer to calm down)

Now, here's what happens when they collide:

You're trying to complete a task (executive function), but you get frustrated (emotion). In a neurotypical brain, executive function would help regulate that frustration. But your executive function is already struggling with the task. The frustration builds (emotional dysregulation), making executive function worse. You might impulsively quit (poor inhibitory control meets emotional reactivity), then feel intense shame (emotional sensitivity), which you can't think your way through (impaired working memory), creating more dysregulation.

It's not that you're not trying hard enough. Your brain is literally fighting itself.

The Precuneus Problem Nobody Talks About

Here's something fascinating that recent research has uncovered: people with BPD show hyperconnectivity in something called the precuneus. Never heard of it? Most people haven't, but it might explain a lot about your experience.

The precuneus is involved in:

- Self-awareness and self-reflection
- Consciousness and sense of self
- Episodic memory retrieval
- Taking others' perspectives

In BPD, this area is hyperconnected to emotional regions. It's like having a hypervigilant sense of self that's constantly checking: "Who am I? How do others see me? What does this mean about me?" Every experience gets processed through this intensely self-referential filter.

Add ADHD to the picture, and things get complicated. ADHD often involves differences in the default mode network (DMN), which includes the precuneus. The DMN is active when you're not focused on the outside world – during daydreaming, self-reflection, or mental time travel.

In ADHD, the DMN doesn't properly "turn off" when you're trying to focus on tasks. It keeps humming in the background, pulling your attention inward. Combine this with BPD's precuneus hyperactivity, and you get:

- Constant, intrusive self-analysis
- Difficulty staying present-focused
- Identity confusion amplified by attention problems
- Rumination that you can't control or stop
- Feeling disconnected from reality while simultaneously hyper-aware of yourself

Reward Centers Gone Haywire

Both ADHD and BPD involve major disruptions in the brain's reward system, but they manifest differently. Understanding this helps explain some of your most frustrating patterns.

The ADHD brain shows reduced activity in reward centers, particularly the ventral striatum. This means:

- Regular rewards don't feel rewarding enough
- You need more intense stimulation to feel satisfied
- Delayed rewards feel almost impossible to work toward
- You might chase novelty because it temporarily activates reward centers

The BPD brain shows irregular reward processing, especially for social rewards. You might:

- Over-respond to positive social feedback
- Under-respond to non-social rewards
- Have trouble learning from reward patterns
- Experience reward and punishment as more intense

When combined, these create unique challenges:

Relationship addiction patterns: Your brain craves the intense reward of new relationships (ADHD novelty-seeking meets BPD attachment needs), but can't sustain the focus and emotional regulation needed for long-term relationships.

Achievement paralysis: You desperately want to accomplish things but can't make yourself do boring preparatory work (ADHD), and the fear of failure triggers emotional dysregulation (BPD), creating a cycle of starting and stopping.

Substance use vulnerability: Both conditions increase addiction risk, but together they create a perfect storm – seeking stimulation (ADHD) to regulate emotions (BPD) with a reward system that doesn't calibrate properly (both).

How Trauma Rewires Everything

Here's something crucial: trauma doesn't just give you bad memories – it literally rewires your brain. And when trauma happens to a brain that's already wired differently (ADHD) or prone to emotional sensitivity (BPD), the effects compound in complex ways.

Trauma affects:

- **The hippocampus** (memory and learning): Often smaller in both ADHD and trauma survivors
- **The amygdala** (fear and emotion): Enlarged and overactive in BPD and PTSD
- **The prefrontal cortex** (executive function): Underactive in ADHD, disrupted by trauma
- **The HPA axis** (stress response system): Dysregulated in both conditions and trauma

But it's not just about structure – it's about how these systems talk to each other. Trauma disrupts the integration between thinking and feeling brains, making it harder to:

- Accurately assess threats
- Regulate emotional responses

- Form coherent narratives about experiences
- Trust your own perceptions
- Feel safe in your body

When you have ADHD, trauma might:

- Make attention problems worse
- Increase hypervigilance that looks like hyperactivity
- Create sensory sensitivities
- Disrupt already fragile executive function

When you have BPD, trauma might:

- Intensify fear of abandonment
- Increase dissociation
- Create more identity fragmentation
- Amplify emotional dysregulation

With both conditions plus trauma, your brain is trying to manage three different levels of disruption. No wonder life feels impossibly hard sometimes.

The Glutamate/GABA Imbalance Story

Now for some cutting-edge science that might explain why your brain feels like it's constantly revving too high or crashing too low.

Glutamate and GABA are your brain's main neurotransmitters:

- **Glutamate** is excitatory – it's the accelerator
- **GABA** is inhibitory – it's the brakes

In a balanced brain, these work together to maintain steady functioning. In ADHD and BPD, this balance is off.

ADHD often involves:

- Lower GABA levels (weak brakes)
- Altered glutamate functioning (inconsistent acceleration)
- Regional imbalances (some areas too excited, others too inhibited)

BPD research suggests:

- Reduced GABA in emotional regulation areas
- Possible glutamate excess in some regions
- Disrupted balance in prefrontal areas

Together, this creates a brain that:

- Can't properly inhibit responses (impulsivity in both conditions)
- Experiences racing thoughts (too much excitation)
- Struggles with emotional and attention regulation (poor inhibition)
- Might feel "wired but tired" (excitation with poor regulation)
- Has trouble with sleep (can't "turn off")

This imbalance might also explain why certain treatments work. Some medications help by:

- Increasing GABA (like certain anxiety medications)
- Modulating glutamate (like some mood stabilizers)
- Improving the balance between them

Your Brain on a Typical Day

Let's walk through what's actually happening in your brain during a regular day with both conditions:

Morning: You wake up. Your ADHD brain is sluggish, needing stimulation to come online. Your BPD brain immediately starts scanning: "How do I feel? What happened yesterday? What threats exist today?" The combination creates morning paralysis – you're simultaneously under-aroused and anxious.

Getting ready: Executive function struggles to sequence tasks (ADHD) while emotional reactions to small frustrations build (BPD). Choosing clothes becomes overwhelming because identity confusion (BPD) meets decision paralysis (ADHD).

Work/school: Your attention drifts (ADHD) until something emotional hooks you (BPD). Then you're hyperfocused on the emotional content while missing important task information. Social interactions trigger intense reactions that your poor working memory can't properly process.

Afternoon crash: Both conditions involve energy regulation problems. ADHD creates inconsistent arousal. BPD emotional storms are exhausting. Together, you hit walls where functioning becomes nearly impossible.

Evening: You're tired but wired. Your brain can't downshift properly (glutamate/GABA imbalance). Emotional review of the day (BPD) meets racing thoughts (ADHD), creating rumination spirals.

Night: Sleep requires nervous system regulation that both conditions disrupt. You're exhausted but can't stop thinking, feeling, planning, worrying.

The Hidden Strengths in Different Wiring

Here's something the textbooks don't emphasize enough: the same brain differences that create struggles also create strengths.

Your ADHD-BPD brain might be:

- **Highly creative**: Divergent thinking (ADHD) plus emotional depth (BPD)

- **Intensely empathetic**: Emotional sensitivity plus hyperawareness of others
- **Pattern recognizers**: Noticing connections others miss
- **Crisis-capable**: Functioning well in high-stimulation situations
- **Passionate**: When interested, nobody engages more deeply
- **Authentic**: Less able to mask means more genuine expression

These aren't consolation prizes. They're real advantages in certain situations. The key is understanding when your different wiring helps and when it hinders, then structuring your life accordingly.

Making Brain Science Practical

Understanding your brain isn't just intellectual exercise – it's the foundation for practical change. When you know what's happening neurologically, you can:

Work with your dopamine system:

- Break tasks into smaller rewards
- Use novelty strategically
- Understand why you need more stimulation
- Stop shaming yourself for seeking intensity

Support executive function:

- External structure compensates for internal struggles
- Visual reminders bypass working memory issues
- Body doubling provides accountability
- Medication can level the playing field

Regulate the emotional storms:

- Know that intense reactions have neurological basis
- Use physical interventions (cold water, exercise) to reset
- Understand why DBT skills are harder for you to implement
- Have compassion for your slower emotional return to baseline

Balance excitation and inhibition:

- Recognize when you need more stimulation vs. calming
- Use activities that increase GABA (yoga, meditation)
- Avoid things that worsen imbalance (excessive caffeine)
- Understand your "wired but tired" states

Your Brain Is Not Your Enemy

After all this brain science, here's the most important thing to understand: your brain is not broken, and it's not your enemy. It's different. It's working with the blueprint it has, trying its best to keep you safe and functional in a world that wasn't designed for brains like yours.

Yes, your brain creates challenges. The emotional storms, the executive dysfunction, the identity confusion, the relationship chaos – these are real and difficult. But your brain also creates the intensity with which you love, the creativity with which you solve problems, the depth with which you experience life.

The goal isn't to have a "normal" brain. The goal is to understand your unique brain well enough to work with it, support it, and build a life that fits its needs. That includes getting proper treatment, which we'll explore in the coming chapters.

Chapter 3: Diagnostic Confusion

Why It Took So Long to Get Answers

Mark's diagnostic journey started when he was seven. "Hyperactive," they said. "Defiant," they added by age ten. "Depression" at fifteen. "Anxiety disorder" at eighteen. "Bipolar II" at twenty-three. "Actually, maybe borderline personality" at twenty-eight. Finally, at thirty-four, after his life had fallen apart for the third time, someone said the words that changed everything: "I think you have both ADHD and borderline personality disorder."

Fifteen years. Four psychiatrists. Six therapists. Thousands of dollars. Countless medications that half-worked or made things worse. And all because the mental health system is terrible at recognizing when someone has both conditions.

Mark's story isn't unique. In fact, it's so common that researchers have started studying the misdiagnosis patterns themselves. What they've found is a system that's almost designed to miss dual diagnoses, sending people on years-long wild goose chases that often make their symptoms worse.

The Misdiagnosis Merry-Go-Round

Let's talk about why this keeps happening. The mental health field loves clean categories. You walk into an office, describe your symptoms, and the professional tries to fit you into a diagnostic box. But here's the problem: **ADHD and BPD symptoms overlap so much that they can look like dozens of other things**.

Take emotional dysregulation. That's a core feature of BPD, right? Well, it's also present in 70% of adults with ADHD. Impulsivity? Central to both conditions. Relationship problems? Check and check. Identity issues? Yep, both again.

So what happens? Clinicians see what they're trained to see. If you go to someone who specializes in mood disorders, suddenly everything looks like bipolar. See someone focused on trauma? Everything's PTSD. Gender plays a huge role too – women are more likely to be diagnosed with BPD while men get labeled with ADHD, even when they have identical symptoms.

The most common misdiagnosis patterns look like this:

The "Just Depression and Anxiety" Path: You seek help for feeling overwhelmed and unable to cope. The obvious symptoms – sadness, worry, panic – get treated. The underlying ADHD and BPD remain invisible. Antidepressants might help a bit, but the core issues persist.

The "Bipolar Disorder" Confusion: Emotional intensity gets mistaken for mania. Impulsivity looks like manic behavior. The inability to maintain stable functioning seems like cycling moods. You get put on mood stabilizers that don't really stabilize anything because the problem isn't actually bipolar disorder.

The "Pure BPD" Diagnosis: All your struggles get attributed to personality issues. The ADHD component is overlooked or dismissed as just part of your emotional dysregulation. You're sent to DBT, which helps but doesn't address the executive function problems making implementation nearly impossible.

The "It's All ADHD" Oversimplification: You get diagnosed with ADHD and everyone assumes that explains everything. Stimulants help with focus but might make emotional symptoms worse. The deeper attachment and identity issues get ignored.

Age of Onset Myths That Keep You Stuck

One of the biggest barriers to accurate diagnosis is the myth about when these conditions "should" appear. Traditional thinking says ADHD starts in childhood and BPD emerges in late adolescence or early adulthood. Therefore, if you're an adult seeking help, clinicians might assume it can't be ADHD, or if you're a teen, it can't be BPD.

But reality is messier than textbooks suggest. ADHD symptoms might have been there all along but were:

- Masked by high intelligence
- Compensated for by family support
- Hidden by anxiety and people-pleasing
- Attributed to "personality" or "temperament"
- Overlooked because you weren't hyperactive

Many adults with ADHD report that their symptoms only became obvious when:

- They left structured environments (school, parents' home)
- Life demands exceeded their coping capacity
- They had children with ADHD and recognized themselves
- Hormonal changes made symptoms worse
- Their compensation strategies stopped working

BPD, supposedly an adult disorder, often has roots that trace back to childhood. Kids who later develop BPD often show:

- Extreme emotional sensitivity from infancy
- Intense separation anxiety
- Difficulty with emotional regulation
- Identity confusion starting early
- Relationship instability with peers

The artificial age cutoffs in diagnostic criteria mean that teenagers with BPD symptoms get labeled with everything except BPD, while adults with lifelong ADHD get told they can't have it because "it would have been caught earlier."

The Screening Tools That Fail You

Standard screening tools are part of the problem. Most are designed to catch one condition or the other, not both. Even worse, they often can't distinguish between them.

Take the Adult ADHD Self-Report Scale (ASRS). It asks about concentration, organization, and restlessness. But guess what? Those symptoms also occur in BPD, especially during emotional distress. If you take this screening when you're emotionally dysregulated, you might score high for ADHD when the real issue is BPD-related cognitive dysfunction.

The McLean Screening Instrument for BPD (MSI-BPD) has the opposite problem. It focuses on emotional symptoms and relationship patterns but doesn't account for how ADHD might influence these. Your fear of abandonment might be intensified by repeatedly losing people due to ADHD-related mistakes. Your impulsivity might be dopamine-seeking rather than emotion-driven.

Even comprehensive assessments miss things. The Minnesota Multiphasic Personality Inventory (MMPI) might show elevation on multiple scales without clearly pointing to either condition. Continuous performance tests for ADHD might be normal if you're motivated or stressed during testing, even though your daily life functioning is impaired.

What's needed – and what rarely happens – is:

- Assessment of both conditions simultaneously
- Understanding how symptoms interact
- Looking at functioning across different contexts
- Considering developmental history comprehensively
- Recognizing masked or compensated symptoms

Finding the Right Diagnostician (The Quest)

Finding someone who can accurately diagnose both conditions is like finding a unicorn. But they exist, and knowing what to look for can save you years of wandering in the diagnostic wilderness.

Red flags to watch for:

- They diagnose you in the first session
- They dismiss either condition without thorough assessment
- They say things like "you can't have ADHD because you finished college"
- They insist BPD is untreatable or just manipulation
- They don't ask about developmental history
- They ignore cultural or gender factors
- They seem unfamiliar with comorbidity research

Green flags to seek:

- They take extensive history (childhood through present)
- They ask about symptoms in different contexts
- They consider how conditions might mask or amplify each other
- They use multiple assessment methods
- They involve collateral information (with your permission)
- They acknowledge diagnostic uncertainty
- They're willing to adjust diagnosis as more information emerges

The best diagnosticians often have:

- Experience with both conditions

- Understanding of neurodevelopmental and personality disorders
- Awareness of gender and cultural factors
- Openness to complex presentations
- Collaborative approach to assessment

Sometimes finding the right person means:

- Seeking specialists in major cities or universities
- Using telehealth to access experts
- Getting separate evaluations then finding someone to integrate them
- Working with a team rather than one provider

Building Your Medical History Timeline

One of the most powerful things you can do is create a comprehensive timeline of your symptoms and life experiences. This helps clinicians see patterns they might otherwise miss.

Start with early childhood:

- What do family members remember about your temperament?
- Were there early signs of sensitivity, hyperactivity, or attention issues?
- What was your academic pattern (smart but underachieving? Perfectionist? Chaotic?)
- How were friendships (intense? unstable? difficulty maintaining?)
- Any early trauma or family chaos?

Move through school years:

- When did struggles become apparent?

- What coping mechanisms did you develop?
- Were there signs others missed ("chatty" instead of hyperactive, "dramatic" instead of dysregulated)?
- What feedback did teachers give?
- When did you first feel "different"?

Document adolescence:

- When did emotional symptoms intensify?
- What triggered the first mental health contact?
- Were there self-harm behaviors? Eating issues? Substance experimentation?
- How did relationships go?
- What diagnoses were given or considered?

Track adulthood patterns:

- What life transitions were hardest?
- When have symptoms been better or worse?
- What treatments have you tried and how did they work?
- What patterns keep repeating?
- What functionality has been lost over time?

Include medical factors:

- Hormonal influences on symptoms
- Head injuries or medical conditions
- Medication responses (what helped, what made things worse)
- Substance use patterns
- Sleep issues throughout life

This timeline becomes invaluable because it:

- Shows patterns across developmental stages
- Reveals both conditions' presence
- Documents failed treatments and why they failed
- Demonstrates functional impairment
- Provides concrete examples

The Questions Nobody Asks But Should

When you're being evaluated, certain questions rarely get asked but could unlock accurate diagnosis. You might need to bring these up yourself:

About attention and executive function:

- "Has anyone ever told me I'm spacey or that I don't listen?"
- "Do I lose things constantly, even important things?"
- "Can I watch a movie without doing something else?"
- "Do I interrupt because thoughts disappear if I don't say them immediately?"
- "Is my living space chaotic despite wanting it clean?"

About emotional patterns:

- "Do my emotions hit faster than I can think?"
- "Does criticism feel like death?"
- "Do I feel empty when I'm not in crisis?"
- "Are my emotions too big for the situations that trigger them?"
- "Do I feel like different people in different relationships?"

About the intersection:

- "Do attention problems get worse when I'm emotional?"
- "Do emotional storms happen when I'm overwhelmed by tasks?"
- "Does rejection make me unable to function for days?"
- "Do I seek chaos when bored but can't handle it when it comes?"
- "Are my relationship problems partly because I forget the good times?"

About compensation and masking:

- "How much energy do I spend appearing 'normal'?"
- "What systems do I have to manage what others do automatically?"
- "How would I function without my coping strategies?"
- "What would others see if I stopped masking for a week?"
- "How different is my internal experience from what I show?"

Why Accurate Diagnosis Actually Matters

You might wonder: if treatment is similar anyway, why does accurate diagnosis matter? Here's why it's crucial:

Medication decisions: ADHD often requires stimulants, which some doctors fear giving to people with BPD. BPD might benefit from mood stabilizers that don't help pure ADHD. Getting both diagnoses ensures access to appropriate medication trials.

Treatment planning: Pure DBT might frustrate someone with ADHD who can't implement skills due to executive dysfunction. Pure ADHD coaching might ignore emotional dysregulation. Dual diagnosis leads to integrated treatment.

Self-understanding: Knowing you have both conditions explains SO much – why some strategies work partially, why you're different from others with just one condition, why your path has been so difficult.

Advocacy and accommodation: You might need workplace accommodations for ADHD and understanding for BPD-related needs. Having official diagnoses helps you advocate for what you need.

Community and support: Finding others with dual diagnosis can be life-changing. You're not alone in this specific struggle.

Insurance and services: Unfortunately, insurance often requires specific diagnoses for coverage. Having both documented can open doors to more comprehensive treatment.

The Relief and Grief of Finally Knowing

When you finally get accurate diagnoses, the emotions can be overwhelming. There's relief – finally, an explanation that makes sense. But there's also grief – for the years lost, the pain that could have been avoided, the life that might have been.

Mark describes it perfectly: "When they told me I had both, I cried for three days. First from relief that I wasn't just 'failing at life.' Then from anger at all the professionals who missed it. Then from grief for my younger self who tried so hard with the wrong tools. Finally, from hope – because now I knew what I was working with."

It's normal to feel:

- Angry at the system that failed you
- Sad for your younger self
- Relieved to have answers
- Scared about what it means
- Hopeful about proper treatment

- Validated in your struggles
- Confused about your identity
- Determined to move forward

Whatever you feel is valid. You've likely spent years being invalidated, misunderstood, and mislabeled. Taking time to process the emotional impact of accurate diagnosis is part of healing.

Creating Your Diagnostic Documentation

Once you have accurate diagnoses, document everything. Create a file that includes:

- Evaluation reports from qualified professionals
- Timeline you created showing both conditions
- List of previous diagnoses and why they didn't fit
- Medication trials and responses
- Functional impairments in different life areas
- How symptoms interact and amplify each other

This documentation serves multiple purposes:

- Prevents future misdiagnosis
- Helps new providers understand quickly
- Supports accommodation requests
- Validates your experience when you doubt yourself
- Shows the journey to accurate diagnosis

Keep both physical and digital copies. Share with trusted supporters. Update as you learn more about how your conditions manifest.

The Path Forward Starts with Knowing

Getting accurate diagnosis of both ADHD and BPD isn't just about labels – it's about finally having a map that matches your actual territory. For possibly the first time in your life, you can stop trying to force yourself into frameworks that don't fit.

Yes, the diagnostic journey is frustrating. The system isn't set up to recognize complex, comorbid conditions. But more professionals are becoming aware of this common combination. Research is expanding. Understanding is growing.

Your job now? Take your accurate diagnoses and use them as tools for building a life that actually works for your unique brain. That means finding treatment that addresses both conditions, which is exactly what we'll explore next.

Chapter 4: The Identity Puzzle

The question hit Jessica like a lightning bolt during a particularly intense therapy session: "Who would I be without my disorders?" She'd been working on "recovery" for years, but suddenly realized she had no idea what that meant. Was she trying to become someone else entirely? Was there a "real" Jessica underneath all the symptoms? Or was she just... this?

For people with both ADHD and BPD, identity isn't just confusing – it's a constantly shifting kaleidoscope where you're never quite sure which patterns are "you" and which are "symptoms." You're the chameleon with racing thoughts, the shape-shifter who can't sit still, the person who feels like everyone and no one all at once.

Two Different Keys, Neither Quite Fitting

The identity challenges in ADHD and BPD are different but equally profound. Understanding both helps explain why you might feel like an alien trying to pass as human.

BPD identity diffusion feels like having no solid core. You might:

- Take on the interests of whoever you're with
- Feel empty when alone
- Drastically change your appearance, goals, or values
- Not know what you want because you want what others want
- Feel like you're performing rather than being

One woman described it: "I'm like water – I take the shape of whatever container I'm in. With my artist friends, I'm creative and spontaneous. With my corporate colleagues, I'm organized and ambitious. Alone, I'm... nothing. Just empty space."

ADHD identity inconsistency is different. You might have a sense of self, but can't maintain it consistently. You might:

- Start hobbies with total conviction, then abandon them
- Make life plans that change every few months
- Feel like different versions of yourself depending on stimulation levels
- Know what you want but can't sustain movement toward it
- Feel authentic but inconsistent

As one man put it: "I know who I am, but I can't stay that person. It's like trying to hold water in my hands – my identity keeps slipping through my fingers."

When you have both, these patterns create a unique challenge. You don't know who you are (BPD) AND can't maintain whoever you decide to be (ADHD). You shape-shift based on others (BPD) but can't sustain even those borrowed identities (ADHD). You might desperately seek yourself while simultaneously losing yourself over and over again.

Values Clarification When Nothing Stays Clear

Traditional values clarification exercises assume you can identify and commit to core values. But what happens when your values feel like they change depending on who you're with, what mood you're in, or what caught your interest this week?

The key is recognizing that your values might be more situational and flexible than traditional models suggest. Instead of seeking fixed values, look for patterns and themes:

What makes you feel alive? Not what you think should matter, but what actually energizes you. Maybe it's intensity, novelty, connection, creativity. These might not be traditional "values," but they're what drive you.

What pain keeps recurring? Sometimes our values are clearer in their violation than their presence. If betrayal devastates you repeatedly, loyalty matters deeply. If boredom feels like death, stimulation is a core need.

What threads persist through all your changes? Even as you shift and change, certain themes probably recur. Maybe you're always drawn to underdogs, always seeking beauty, always fighting injustice, even if the form changes.

What would you fight for even when dysregulated? In your worst moments, what still matters? This might be your truest value – what survives even emotional storms and executive dysfunction.

Instead of a fixed value system, you might develop what I call a "values constellation" – a flexible arrangement of principles that can shift position but remain present. Some days creativity is your north star, other days it's connection. The constellation remains even as its orientation changes.

Career Confusion and Multiple Interests

Career development with ADHD-BPD is like trying to build a house on shifting sand during an earthquake. The traditional model – pick a path, develop expertise, climb the ladder – might feel impossible or like prison.

Your career challenges might include:

- **Serial obsessions**: Becoming utterly consumed with a field, then losing all interest
- **Identity through work**: Needing career to provide identity you can't internally generate
- **Performance anxiety**: Fearing failure so much you don't try, or trying so hard you burn out
- **Interpersonal chaos**: Leaving jobs due to relationship conflicts or perceived rejections

- **Impostor syndrome on steroids**: Not just feeling fake, but not knowing what "real" would be

But here's a reframe: maybe you're not meant for a traditional career path. Maybe your brain is built for:

Portfolio careers: Multiple income streams that satisfy different aspects of yourself. When interest in one wanes, others sustain you.

Project-based work: Intense, time-limited engagements that match your intensity cycles. You can be fully invested without lifetime commitment.

Cyclical careers: Rotating between different types of work based on your current functioning and interests. Seasonal work, contract rotations, deliberate variety.

Mission-driven work: Finding an overarching purpose that can be expressed through various roles. The mission stays stable even as the form changes.

Creative entrepreneurship: Building something that can flex with your fluctuations. Your business becomes an extension of your changing self rather than a fixed structure you must maintain.

The key is stopping the shame about not having a "normal" career and starting to build something that actually works with your neurodiversity.

Building Stable Self-Concept with Inherent Instability

How do you build a stable sense of self when instability is literally part of your neurology? The answer isn't to become stable – it's to become comfortable with fluidity while maintaining some core threads.

Think of identity like a jazz performance rather than a classical composition. Jazz has structure – key signatures, rhythm patterns, recurring themes – but also improvisation, variation, spontaneous creation. You're not supposed to play the same song the same way every time.

Create identity anchors: These aren't fixed personality traits but rather touchpoints you can return to:

- Physical objects that remind you who you are
- Photos documenting your journey
- Journals showing your evolution
- Playlists that capture different aspects of yourself
- Relationships with people who've known you over time

Document your patterns: Since your memory might be unreliable (ADHD) and your self-perception shifts (BPD), external documentation helps:

- Keep a "self-observation journal"
- Track what interests persist vs. pass
- Notice what triggers identity shifts
- Record what feels authentic vs. performed
- Document what others consistently see in you

Embrace your multiplicity: Instead of seeking one "true self," acknowledge your legitimate multiple selves:

- Professional you
- Creative you
- Crisis you
- Intimate relationship you
- Alone you
- Stimulated you

- Understimulated you

These are all real. The goal isn't integration into one self but rather coordination among your various selves.

Create continuity rituals: Since you can't rely on internal continuity, create external ones:

- Morning routines that remind you who you are
- Weekly check-ins with yourself
- Monthly reviews of your journey
- Seasonal celebrations of growth
- Annual letters to future you

Negative Identity and Stigma Navigation

Both ADHD and BPD carry massive stigma, and having both means navigating a minefield of negative assumptions. You might have internalized messages that you're:

- Manipulative (BPD stereotype)
- Lazy (ADHD stereotype)
- Attention-seeking (BPD)
- Careless (ADHD)
- Unstable (BPD)
- Unreliable (ADHD)
- Toxic (BPD)
- Immature (ADHD)

These stereotypes can become what's called "negative identity" – defining yourself by what you're told is wrong with you. You might think, "I'm the chaotic one," "I'm the crazy ex," "I'm the family problem," "I'm the one who ruins everything."

Challenging negative identity requires:

Recognizing that symptoms aren't character flaws. Emotional dysregulation isn't manipulation. Executive dysfunction isn't laziness. These are neurobiological differences, not moral failings.

Separating behavior from identity. You might have done harmful things while dysregulated or impulsive. That doesn't make you a harmful person. You're a person with neurological differences navigating a world not built for your brain.

Finding counter-narratives. For every "borderline manipulation" story, there are people with BPD showing incredible empathy. For every "ADHD failure" narrative, there are people with ADHD creating innovative solutions. Find these stories. Join these communities.

Creating affirming language. Instead of "I'm borderline," try "I have BPD." Instead of "I'm so ADHD," try "My ADHD is active today." You are not your diagnoses.

Setting boundaries around stigma. You don't owe anyone education about your conditions. You don't have to tolerate stigmatizing language. You can choose who gets to know about your diagnoses and how much they know.

The Shape-Shifter's Dilemma

Many people with BPD-ADHD describe themselves as shape-shifters, constantly adapting to their environment. This isn't necessarily pathological – it might be an evolutionary adaptation. In unpredictable, invalidating, or dangerous environments, being able to quickly read and match others is survival.

But it creates unique challenges:

You might not know which thoughts/feelings are yours vs. absorbed from others. In a room full of people, you're feeling everyone's emotions plus your own, filtered through ADHD's difficulty sorting relevant from irrelevant information.

You lose yourself in relationships. It's not just codependency – your brain literally syncs with others more intensely. Mirror neurons on overdrive. You become who they need, then forget who you were before.

Solo time feels empty but necessary. You need space to reset to baseline, but baseline feels like nothingness. The ADHD needs stimulation, the BPD fears abandonment, and solitude triggers both.

Authenticity feels dangerous. If you've survived by shape-shifting, being "yourself" can feel like exposure, vulnerability, potential rejection. But not being yourself maintains the exhausting performance.

Working with shape-shifting rather than against it might involve:

- Conscious choosing when and how much to adapt
- Regular "identity inventory" to track what's yours vs. absorbed
- Relationships with people who appreciate your fluidity
- Careers that utilize your adaptability
- Scheduled "self time" to reconnect with your core
- Practicing small acts of authenticity to build tolerance

Identity and Medication

Here's something rarely discussed: medication can create identity confusion. When stimulants help your ADHD, you might wonder, "Is this the 'real' me or the 'medicated' me?" When mood stabilizers reduce BPD symptoms, you might grieve the intensity that felt like part of your identity.

Common medication-related identity questions:

- "Am I only creative when unmedicated?"
- "Is my personality just brain chemistry?"

- "Who am I without my intensity?"
- "Are my achievements only possible with medication?"
- "Do people like medicated or unmedicated me?"

There's no easy answer, but consider this: Glasses don't make you "fake-sighted." They help you see what was always there. Similarly, medication doesn't create a false you – it might reveal aspects of you that were hidden by symptom noise.

Some find it helpful to think of medication as:

- A tool that helps you access more of your range
- A support that lets your intentions match your actions
- A filter that reduces static so your signal comes through
- A bridge between who you are and who you want to be

The "real you" includes all versions – medicated, unmedicated, regulated, dysregulated. The question isn't which is real but rather which helps you live according to your values and goals.

Building Identity Through Relationships

Relationships are both the challenge and potential solution for identity with BPD-ADHD. They trigger your symptoms AND potentially provide the stability you can't internally generate.

Challenges include:

- Losing yourself in others (BPD)
- Forgetting relationship history (ADHD)
- Intensity that overwhelms others (both)
- Inconsistency that confuses others (both)
- Fear that keeps you from being known (BPD)
- Distraction that prevents deep connection (ADHD)

But relationships can also provide:

- External continuity when internal is impossible
- Mirrors that reflect consistent aspects of you
- Memory keepers who remember your journey
- Reality checks when perception distorts
- Co-regulation when self-regulation fails
- Identity through role (friend, partner, parent)

The key is finding relationships that can hold your complexity without trying to simplify you. People who can say, "I see all your selves and value them all." People who remember who you are when you forget.

Cultural Identity Complications

If you're from a marginalized culture, identity formation is even more complex. You're navigating:

- Cultural identity vs. diagnostic identity
- Collective self vs. individual self
- Traditional healing vs. Western medicine
- Family identity vs. personal identity
- Cultural stigma plus diagnostic stigma

You might wonder: Are my struggles from trauma, culture, neurodiversity, or all three? Is my emotional intensity cultural expression or BPD? Is my different thinking style ADHD or bilingual/bicultural brain?

There's no need to parse it perfectly. You can be both/and:

- Culturally expressive AND have BPD
- Bilingual creative thinking AND ADHD

- Trauma survivor AND neurodivergent
- Connected to tradition AND seeking treatment

Your identity doesn't have to fit Western psychological models. You can create your own integration of cultural identity, lived experience, and neurodiversity.

Becoming Who You're Becoming

Here's the truth about identity with ADHD and BPD: You might never have the solid, consistent sense of self that neurotypical people take for granted. And that's okay.

Your identity might always be more fluid, contextual, multiple. You might always feel like you're becoming rather than being. You might never fully answer "Who am I?" in a permanent way.

But maybe that's not pathology – maybe it's possibility. Maybe your brain is designed for adaptation, evolution, continuous becoming. Maybe in a rapidly changing world, fluid identity is an advantage.

The goal isn't to fix your identity into place but to become comfortable with its fluidity. To build enough structure to function while maintaining enough flexibility to grow. To know yourself as a verb rather than a noun – not who you are but how you are, how you move through the world, how you connect and create and survive and thrive.

Your multifaceted identity isn't a problem to solve. It's a complex gift that requires different management than simpler identities. You're not broken or fragmented – you're multiple, adaptive, evolving. And with the right support and understanding, you can build a life that honors all aspects of who you are and who you're becoming.

Section II: Treatment That Actually Works
Evidence-Based Approaches for Dual Diagnosis

Chapter 5: DBT Meets ADHD

Skills Training That Sticks

Jessica sat in the DBT group for the fourth time, watching everyone else diligently fill out their diary cards while her mind pinged between seventeen different thoughts. The therapist was explaining emotion regulation... again. Jessica knew the concepts. Hell, she could probably teach them at this point. PLEASE skills, TIPP, wise mind – she'd memorized it all. But knowing and doing? That gap felt like the Grand Canyon.

"I get it intellectually," she'd told her individual therapist earlier that week. "But when I'm dysregulated, my brain just... leaves. Like, the skills are in there somewhere, but I can't find them. It's like trying to find your keys when the house is on fire and also you have amnesia."

Her therapist leaned back, considering. "Jessica, has anyone ever adapted these DBT skills specifically for your ADHD brain?"

The question changed everything. For the next six months, Jessica worked with a therapist who understood both conditions. They didn't just teach DBT – they translated it for her ADHD-BPD brain. They created visual cues, simplified steps, built in dopamine hits, and acknowledged that her executive dysfunction wasn't resistance or self-sabotage.

By 35, Jessica finally learned emotional regulation. Not perfect regulation, not neurotypical regulation, but HER regulation. And it stuck.

Why Standard DBT Only Gets You Halfway

Dialectical Behavior Therapy is the gold standard for treating BPD. It works. Studies show that 77% of people who complete DBT no longer meet criteria for BPD after a year. But here's what those studies don't highlight: completion rates are often below 50%, and people with ADHD are significantly more likely to drop out.

Why? Because DBT was designed for BPD brains, not ADHD-BPD brains. It assumes certain cognitive capabilities that ADHD specifically impairs:

- Consistent attention during 2.5-hour group sessions
- Working memory to hold multiple skill concepts
- Executive function to implement homework
- Sequential processing to follow skill steps
- Sustained motivation through repetitive practice

Standard DBT is like being given an incredibly sophisticated smartphone with a dead battery. All that functionality is there, but you can't access it when you need it.

The four modules of DBT – mindfulness, distress tolerance, emotion regulation, and interpersonal effectiveness – are exactly what you need. But the delivery system needs serious modification to work with your dual diagnosis.

Adapting DBT for Executive Dysfunction

Executive dysfunction isn't just forgetting to do homework or losing diary cards (though that happens too). It's a fundamental difference in how your brain processes, stores, and retrieves information. When you add emotional dysregulation to the mix, standard DBT teaching methods hit a wall.

Here's how to adapt each component:

Skill Instruction Adaptations:

Instead of lecturing for 45 minutes, break content into 10-minute chunks. Your ADHD brain checks out after about 10 minutes anyway, so work with it, not against it. Between chunks, do something physical

– stretch, walk around the room, do jumping jacks. Movement resets attention.

Use visual aids for everything. Not just handouts – actual visual representations. Emotion regulation becomes a thermometer you can see. Distress tolerance becomes a ladder you climb down. Interpersonal effectiveness becomes a flow chart. Your brain processes visual information faster and retains it better than verbal instruction.

Create acronyms that actually stick. PLEASE is good, but what about STOP FEAR for crisis moments:

- **S**top what you're doing
- **T**ake a breath
- **O**bserve your body
- **P**ick one skill
- **F**ocus on just that
- **E**xecute it imperfectly
- **A**ccept good enough
- **R**epeat if needed

Homework Adaptations:

Forget traditional diary cards with their tiny boxes and overwhelming options. Create a simplified version:

- Three emotions max per day
- Scale of 1-5 for intensity
- One skill used (doesn't matter if it worked)
- One word describing the day

Better yet, use technology. Apps, voice memos, photo logs – whatever captures information in the moment. Your ADHD brain won't remember to fill things out later, so capture data immediately.

Make homework into a game. Seriously. Give yourself points for using skills. Create achievements to unlock. "Used TIPP three times this week? You've earned the Ice Master badge!" It sounds silly, but your dopamine-seeking brain needs rewards, and BPD makes external validation even more reinforcing.

Making Skills Stick with ADHD Memory Issues

The biggest challenge with DBT and ADHD isn't learning the skills – it's remembering they exist when you need them. Your working memory is already impaired, and emotional dysregulation makes it worse. In crisis, your brain goes offline, and all those carefully learned skills vanish like smoke.

The solution? External memory aids that don't require internal recall:

Physical Anchors:

Wear a bracelet with skill reminders. Not just "DBT" but actual skill cues. Different colored beads for different skills. Touch the red bead = STOP skill. Blue = TIPP. When you're dysregulated, you might not remember skills exist, but you'll notice the bracelet.

Create skill cards for your wallet. Not lengthy explanations – just bullet points:

- Feeling overwhelming emotion?
- Put face in cold water
- Or hold ice cubes
- Or do jumping jacks
- Pick one. Do it now.

Environmental Cues:

Put sticky notes where you'll see them during crisis. On the bathroom mirror: "Splash cold water on face." On the refrigerator: "Eat something with protein." On your phone lock screen: "Text your accountability buddy."

Create a crisis kit that's always in the same place. Bright red box labeled "EMERGENCY SKILLS." Inside: ice pack, rubber band, strong mints, stress ball, printed skill cards, playlist of calming music, photos that ground you. When dysregulated, you don't have to remember skills – just remember the red box.

Technology Assists:

Set random skill reminders on your phone. Not "practice DBT" but specific actions: "Check in with your body right now." "Rate your emotion 1-10." "Take three deep breaths." These pop up throughout the day, building skill habit when you're calm so they're more accessible during crisis.

Use voice memos to coach yourself through skills. Record yourself when calm, talking yourself through TIPP or PLEASE. During crisis, you just have to press play and follow your own voice.

PLEASE Skills for Physical Vulnerability

PLEASE skills address physical vulnerability factors that make emotional dysregulation worse. For ADHD-BPD brains, these are absolutely crucial because both conditions affect physical regulation:

Physical illness - Treat it
Live healthy - Balance eating
Exercise - Do some daily
Avoid mood-altering substances
Sleep - Get enough
Eat - Don't skip meals

But here's the thing: ADHD makes every single one of these harder. You forget to take medication. Hyperfocus makes you skip meals.

Executive dysfunction sabotages exercise routines. Time blindness destroys sleep schedules. And both conditions increase substance use risk.

So let's make PLEASE skills ADHD-friendly:

Physical Illness: Set medication alarms that won't turn off until you scan a QR code placed next to your meds. Use pill organizers with built-in timers. Track symptoms in a one-click app, not a journal. Partner with someone for accountability – body doubling works for healthcare too.

Live Healthy/Balance Eating: Forget perfect nutrition. Focus on "good enough" eating. Keep protein shakes, meal bars, and pre-cut vegetables always available. When executive function is shot, eating something is better than eating nothing. Set alarms for meals. Put "EAT" on your calendar like an appointment.

Exercise: Don't commit to a gym routine you'll abandon in two weeks. Instead, focus on movement that provides immediate reward. Dance to one song. Do pushups during commercial breaks. Walk around the block when restless. The goal isn't fitness – it's emotional regulation through movement.

Avoid Substances: This is tough because both conditions increase addiction risk, and substances often provide short-term relief. Instead of "just say no," focus on harm reduction and replacement. If you smoke when stressed, try substituting with intense exercise or cold water. If you drink to calm down, experiment with weighted blankets or ASMR videos. Track patterns between substance use and emotional storms – data helps your logical brain support your emotional brain.

Sleep: Your ADHD brain doesn't want to sleep, and your BPD brain catastrophizes at 3 AM. Create an elaborate wind-down routine that starts 2 hours before bed. Set alarms for starting routine, not just bedtime. Use sleep stories, white noise, weighted blankets – whatever helps. And when you can't sleep? Have a plan that doesn't involve scrolling your phone and spiraling.

Eat: Keep "emergency food" everywhere – car, desk, bag, jacket pockets. When you notice you're getting irritable or spacey, eat something immediately. Don't wait to figure out what you "should" eat. Crackers in the moment beat a balanced meal never eaten.

Distress Tolerance for Dual Crisis Patterns

Crisis with ADHD-BPD isn't like crisis with just one condition. ADHD impulsivity meets BPD desperation, creating a perfect storm where you're simultaneously unable to think clearly AND feeling like you'll die if you don't act immediately. Standard distress tolerance skills need serious adaptation.

The TIPP Skill on Steroids:

Temperature - But make it extreme. Not just cold water on wrists – full face immersion. Ice packs on neck. Cold shower. Your nervous system needs shocking to reset.

Intense Exercise - But shorter bursts. ADHD brain can't sustain 20 minutes of exercise during crisis. Do 30 seconds of maximum intensity. Sprint, not marathon.

Paced Breathing - But with movement. Walking meditation, not sitting. Count steps while breathing. Your hyperactive body needs to move while your breath slows.

Progressive Muscle Relaxation - But faster. Instead of slowly tensing and releasing each muscle group, do full-body tension for 5 seconds, then complete release. Repeat 3 times. Quick and effective.

Crisis Survival Skills Modified:

Standard DBT says distract with activities. But your ADHD brain might hyperfocus on the wrong activity and avoid the issue for weeks. Instead, use **time-limited distraction**: Set a timer for 20 minutes. Distract completely. When timer goes off, check in with yourself. Still in crisis? Another 20 minutes. This prevents both rumination and avoidance.

Self-soothing with five senses works, but make it intense enough to compete with your symptoms:

- **Vision**: Not just looking at something pleasant – watch rapid-movement videos, strobe lights, or optical illusions
- **Hearing**: Not soft music – binaural beats, heavy bass, or complex soundscapes
- **Smell**: Not gentle lavender – peppermint oil, vinegar, or coffee grounds
- **Taste**: Not just candy – extremely sour, spicy, or minty
- **Touch**: Not just soft textures – ice, rough surfaces, or pressure

Radical Acceptance with ADHD Accommodations:

Radical acceptance requires sustained attention and working memory – exactly what you don't have during crisis. So break it down:

1. Accept THIS MOMENT only (not the situation, just this single moment)
2. Say out loud: "Right now, this is happening"
3. Notice fighting it makes it worse
4. Choose to stop fighting for 10 seconds
5. Repeat

Don't try to radically accept your entire life situation. Just this moment. Then the next. ADHD-sized chunks of acceptance.

Interpersonal Effectiveness with Rejection Sensitivity

Rejection Sensitive Dysphoria (RSD) is common in ADHD and makes BPD abandonment fears exponentially worse. Standard interpersonal effectiveness skills help, but need major modifications for your dual rejection sensitivity.

DEAR MAN with RSD Modifications:

Describe - But write it out first. RSD makes you emotional immediately. Script your description when calm.

Express - Own your extreme sensitivity. "I know my reaction seems big, but this is genuinely how it feels to me."

Assert - But softly. Your intensity might overwhelm others. Practice in mirror to modulate.

Reinforce - Focus on mutual benefit, not just what you need. RSD makes you forget others have needs too.

Mindful - Stay focused despite racing thoughts. Have your script visible.

Appear Confident - Even though RSD makes you feel worthless. Power pose before conversation.

Negotiate - But know your walk-away point in advance. RSD makes you give up everything to avoid rejection.

GIVE Skills for Maintaining Relationships:

Gentle - Extra gentle because your RSD might make you aggressive when hurt

Interested - Actually listen despite ADHD urge to interrupt

Validate - Even when your BPD is screaming that they're wrong

Easy Manner - Despite wanting to flee (RSD) or cling (BPD)

FAST Skills for Self-Respect:

Fair - To yourself too, not just others (RSD makes you unfair to yourself)

Apologies - Only for actual wrongs, not for existing

Stick to Values - Write them down because you'll forget when emotional

Truthful - Including about your limitations and needs

Modified DBT Diary Cards That Actually Work

Standard DBT diary cards are overwhelming for ADHD brains. Too many boxes, too many options, too much to remember. Here's a simplified version that captures essential information without triggering executive dysfunction:

Daily Check-In (One Minute Max):

Morning Mood: 😊 😐 ☹️ 😠 (circle one) Evening Mood: 😊 😐 ☹️ 😠 (circle one)

Biggest Challenge Today: _____

Skill I Tried: _____

Did It Help? Y / N / Kinda

Meds Taken? Y / N

Slept? Y / N / Badly

Ate? Y / N / Forgot

One Word for Today: _____

That's it. No 0-10 scales for seventeen different emotions. No tracking every skill used. Just the bare minimum to notice patterns.

Weekly Pattern Review:

Instead of daily detailed tracking, do a weekly pattern review:

- Which day was hardest? Why?
- Which skill got used most?
- What triggered the biggest emotion?

- What helped most?
- What do I need next week?

This captures patterns without overwhelming daily tracking.

Finding DBT Groups That Understand ADHD

Not all DBT groups are created equal, and many aren't prepared for ADHD adaptations. Here's how to find or create what you need:

Questions to Ask Before Joining:

- Can I stand or move during group if needed?
- Are breaks built into the session?
- Can I use fidget tools?
- Is there flexibility on homework format?
- How do you handle attention difficulties?
- Can I record sessions for review?

Red Flags:

- "You just need to try harder"
- Inflexible about traditional diary cards
- No breaks in 2+ hour sessions
- Punishment for missing homework
- Treating ADHD symptoms as "resistance"

Green Flags:

- Multiple learning modalities used
- Movement incorporated
- Flexible homework options
- Understanding of executive dysfunction

- Shorter skill explanations
- Visual aids and handouts

If you can't find an ADHD-friendly DBT group, consider:

- Individual DBT adapted for ADHD
- Online groups with more flexibility
- Creating your own practice group
- Combining DBT with ADHD coaching

Skills That Work Better with Both Conditions

Some DBT skills actually work BETTER when you have both conditions because they address overlapping symptoms:

Opposite Action works for both ADHD procrastination and BPD emotion-driven behavior. Can't start a task (ADHD)? Do one tiny piece. Wanting to rage-text your ex (BPD)? Write the text but don't send it.

Check the Facts helps both ADHD distorted thinking and BPD emotional reasoning. Your brain lies to you in multiple ways – this skill catches all of them.

Accumulate Positive Experiences feeds both your dopamine-seeking ADHD brain and validation-needing BPD brain. Plan small pleasures throughout the day.

Build Mastery addresses both ADHD need for stimulation and BPD need for identity. Learn something new regularly, even if you don't stick with it forever.

Cope Ahead helps both ADHD planning deficits and BPD emotional preparation. Visualize handling situations before they happen.

Making DBT Work for Your Unique Brain

Here's the truth: DBT is incredibly effective for BPD, and it can be equally effective for BPD with ADHD – if it's properly adapted. The skills themselves don't need to change, but the delivery system absolutely does.

Your brain needs:

- Shorter bursts of learning
- Multiple sensory inputs
- Immediate rewards
- External memory aids
- Movement and stimulation
- Simplified tracking systems
- Flexibility in implementation

This isn't dumbing down DBT – it's translating it for your neurodiversity. You're not failing at DBT if standard methods don't work. The methods are failing you.

The goal isn't to do DBT perfectly. It's to use DBT skills effectively for YOUR brain. That might mean your diary card is a voice memo, your mindfulness includes movement, and your distress tolerance looks like controlled chaos. That's not just okay – it's exactly right.

Chapter 6: Medication Matters - Stimulants, Safety, and Stability

David stood in his psychiatrist's office, holding two prescription bottles, feeling like his entire life was about to change. After years of mood stabilizers that didn't stabilize, antidepressants that didn't lift depression, and antipsychotics that made him feel like a zombie, someone had finally said the words: "Let's try treating both conditions."

One bottle contained methylphenidate for his ADHD. The other, lamotrigine for his BPD mood symptoms. His psychiatrist had spent an hour discussing how they'd monitor both, adjust as needed, and watch for interactions. For the first time in his adult life, David had hope that medication might actually help rather than just sedate.

Three months later, he described it to his therapy group: "It wasn't like magic. It was like... someone cleaned my windshield. I could finally see where I was going. The emotions were still there, but I could think through them. The chaos was still there, but I could organize it. For the first time, my brain felt like it was working WITH me instead of against me."

The Medication Controversy No One Wants to Talk About

Here's what nobody tells you: the psychiatric community is terrified of giving stimulants to people with BPD. They worry about addiction, impulsivity, self-harm, and destabilization. Meanwhile, they're comfortable prescribing antipsychotics with severe side effects for off-label BPD treatment. Make it make sense.

Recent research is challenging these fears. A groundbreaking study of 2.3 million Swedish patients found that ADHD medications reduced psychiatric hospitalizations in BPD patients by 12%. Another study showed stimulants decreased self-harm behaviors in people with both conditions. Yet many psychiatrists still refuse to prescribe them.

The reluctance stems from several myths:

- **"Stimulants increase impulsivity"** - Actually, they improve impulse control when ADHD is present
- **"People with BPD will abuse them"** - Addiction risk exists but is manageable with proper monitoring
- **"Stimulants worsen emotional dysregulation"** - They can, initially, but often improve it long-term
- **"It's too dangerous with self-harm history"** - Untreated ADHD may pose greater risk

The reality? Leaving ADHD untreated in someone with BPD might be more dangerous than carefully monitored stimulant treatment.

How Stimulants Actually Affect BPD Symptoms

This might surprise you: stimulants often improve BPD symptoms, not just ADHD ones. Here's why:

Improved Executive Function Helps Emotional Regulation: When you can think clearly, you can use DBT skills. When you can plan, you're less likely to act impulsively on emotions. When you can focus, you're not as overwhelmed by emotional stimuli.

Reduced Chaos Decreases Triggers: Much of what triggers BPD episodes might actually be ADHD-related failures. Lost jobs, ruined relationships, forgotten commitments – these create the instability that activates BPD symptoms. Treat the ADHD, reduce the chaos, decrease the triggers.

Better Decision-Making Under Stress: Research shows methylphenidate improves decision-making in people with BPD, particularly under stress. It helps the prefrontal cortex stay online when emotions surge.

Decreased Rejection Sensitivity: Many people report that stimulants reduce their rejection sensitive dysphoria. Since RSD overlaps with BPD abandonment fears, this can significantly improve relationships.

Stabilized Energy and Mood: The rollercoaster of ADHD energy crashes can trigger BPD mood instability. Steady dopamine from medication creates a more stable baseline.

But (there's always a but), stimulants can also:

- Initially increase anxiety
- Cause emotional blunting at high doses
- Trigger irritability during wearing-off periods
- Create rebound symptoms if stopped suddenly
- Potentially trigger mania in misdiagnosed bipolar

Safety Protocols for High-Risk Patients

Having a history of self-harm or suicidality doesn't automatically disqualify you from stimulant treatment, but it does require extra safeguards:

Start Low, Go Slow: Begin with the lowest possible dose. Increase by tiny increments. Your sensitive system needs time to adjust. What others might increase weekly, you might increase monthly.

Daily Dispensing Initially: Some doctors start with daily or weekly prescriptions rather than monthly. Yes, it's inconvenient. But it prevents impulsive overdose during crisis and helps establish the medication routine.

Regular Check-Ins: Weekly appointments initially, then biweekly, then monthly. These aren't just medication checks – they're stability monitoring. Document mood, self-harm urges, and impulsivity.

Safety Plan Updates: Your crisis plan needs updating to include medication considerations:

- What to do if you feel like overdosing
- Who holds extra medication during crisis
- How to handle missed doses
- When to contact prescriber immediately

Medication Contract: Some psychiatrists use formal agreements outlining:

- Single pharmacy use
- No early refills
- Regular drug testing
- Pill counts if needed
- Immediate reporting of problems

Support System Involvement: With your permission, involving trusted people who can:

- Hold medication if you're unsafe
- Notice concerning changes
- Support medication compliance
- Provide feedback to prescriber

These might feel infantilizing, but they're temporary scaffolding while establishing safety. Most people graduate to standard monitoring within 3-6 months.

The Mood Stabilizer Question

Many people with BPD-ADHD benefit from mood stabilizers alongside or instead of stimulants. The evidence is mixed but promising:

Lamotrigine shows particular promise for BPD, especially for anger and affective instability. It doesn't treat ADHD but might make stimulants more tolerable by stabilizing the emotional baseline. The slow titration is annoying but necessary to avoid dangerous rash.

Valproic Acid can help with aggression and mood swings. Some studies show improvement in impulsivity too. Weight gain and other side effects can be problematic.

Topiramate might help with both emotional dysregulation and ADHD symptoms. Some people report improved focus alongside mood stabilization. The "dopamax" cognitive effects are real for some people though.

Lithium is less commonly used but can help with suicidality and severe mood instability. Requires regular blood monitoring and has a narrow therapeutic window.

Atypical Antipsychotics like quetiapine or aripiprazole are often prescribed but should be carefully considered. They can help with severe dysregulation but carry significant side effect risks and don't address ADHD at all.

The combination approach often works best:

- Stimulant for ADHD symptoms
- Mood stabilizer for emotional baseline
- As-needed medication for acute crisis
- Antidepressant if depression persists

But everyone's cocktail is different. What works for someone else might be terrible for you.

Managing Side Effects When Everything Affects You More

Both ADHD and BPD can make you more sensitive to medication side effects. What others barely notice might be intolerable for you. Common challenges and solutions:

Emotional Blunting: "I don't feel like myself" is common, especially with higher stimulant doses. Solutions:

- Lower the dose
- Switch medications (methylphenidate vs amphetamine)
- Add bupropion for emotional range
- Take medication breaks on low-demand days

Increased Anxiety: Stimulants can initially spike anxiety. Management strategies:

- Start with even lower doses
- Use long-acting formulations for smoother coverage
- Add L-theanine or magnesium
- Practice anxiety management skills before starting
- Consider guanfacine or clonidine as alternatives

Appetite Suppression: Forgetting to eat worsens both conditions. Strategies:

- Set eating alarms
- Liquid nutrition when solid food is impossible
- Eat before medication kicks in
- Keep easy snacks everywhere
- Monitor weight weekly

Sleep Disruption: Both conditions already affect sleep. Medication can make it worse:

- Take stimulants early
- Avoid afternoon doses
- Use melatonin (with prescriber approval)

- Maintain rigid sleep hygiene
- Consider switching to shorter-acting formulations

Rebound/Wearing Off: The afternoon crash can trigger emotional storms:

- Overlap doses slightly
- Use combination immediate/extended release
- Plan low-demand activities for crash times
- Have coping strategies ready for vulnerable periods

Finding a Psychiatrist Who Gets It

Finding a psychiatrist who understands both conditions AND is willing to prescribe appropriately is like finding a unicorn. But they exist. Here's how to find them:

Where to Look:

- ADHD specialty clinics often understand comorbidities
- University/teaching hospitals have updated treatment approaches
- DBT programs might have psychiatrists familiar with dual diagnosis
- Addiction psychiatry (they understand complex medication management)
- Telehealth expands your options significantly

Interview Questions:

- "How often do you treat people with both ADHD and BPD?"
- "What's your approach to stimulants with self-harm history?"
- "How do you monitor for both safety and effectiveness?"

- "Are you willing to work with my therapist?"
- "What's your philosophy on combination medication?"

Red Flags:
- "I never prescribe stimulants to people with BPD"
- "You have to choose which condition to treat"
- "BPD is just severe ADHD" (or vice versa)
- "Medication doesn't help personality disorders"
- "Try therapy first" (when you've been in therapy for years)
- Unwillingness to coordinate with your treatment team

Green Flags:
- Asks detailed questions about both conditions
- Discusses risks honestly without fear-mongering
- Proposes comprehensive monitoring plan
- Willing to start conservatively
- Acknowledges the evidence for treating both
- Respects your expertise about your own experience

The Methylphenidate Decision-Making Study

Here's some fascinating science: researchers found that methylphenidate specifically improves decision-making in people with BPD. Using complex decision-making tasks, they showed that methylphenidate:

- Reduced impulsive choices
- Improved planning ability
- Decreased emotional interference in decisions

- Enhanced learning from consequences

This wasn't just about ADHD symptoms. Even people with BPD without ADHD showed improvement. The medication seems to strengthen the prefrontal cortex's ability to override emotional impulses.

What this means practically: stimulants might help you make better choices during emotional moments. That relationship decision, that impulsive purchase, that self-harm urge – medication might give you just enough cognitive control to choose differently.

Creating Your Medication Monitoring System

You can't rely on memory or subjective feeling to track medication effects. Both conditions affect self-awareness. You need objective tracking:

Daily Tracking (Keep it simple):

- Medication taken: dose and time
- Mood: 1-10 scale, morning and evening
- Focus: 1-10 scale
- Impulsivity: Any major impulses/actions
- Side effects: Note any
- Sleep: Hours and quality

Weekly Review:

- Average mood stability
- Productive days vs lost days
- Relationship conflicts
- Self-harm urges/actions
- Overall functioning

Monthly Patterns:

- Compare to pre-medication baseline
- Note any cycling patterns
- Identify trigger interactions
- Assess overall trajectory

Use apps, spreadsheets, or paper – whatever you'll actually use consistently. Share summaries with your prescriber. Data beats subjective reporting every time.

When Medication Is and Isn't The Answer

Medication can be life-changing for ADHD-BPD, but it's not magic. Realistic expectations:

Medication CAN:

- Improve focus and executive function
- Reduce emotional intensity somewhat
- Decrease impulsivity
- Stabilize energy levels
- Make therapy more effective
- Reduce some triggers

Medication CAN'T:

- Fix trauma
- Replace skill building
- Solve relationship problems
- Cure either condition
- Work without other treatment

- Make you neurotypical

Think of medication as leveling the playing field. If life is a video game, neurotypical people play on easy mode. You've been playing on extreme difficulty. Medication doesn't put you on easy mode – maybe it gets you to hard or medium. You still need skills, support, and strategy.

The Integration Challenge

The biggest challenge isn't finding the right medication – it's integrating medication into comprehensive treatment. Medication without therapy is incomplete. Therapy without medication (when needed) is harder than necessary.

Your treatment team needs coordination:

- Psychiatrist managing medications
- Therapist providing skills and processing
- Primary care monitoring physical health
- You as the CEO of your treatment

Everyone needs to communicate. Therapist notices increased anxiety? Psychiatrist needs to know. Medication change? Therapist needs to adjust expectations. You notice patterns? Everyone needs the information.

Your Medication Journey Is Unique

The path to finding the right medication combination for ADHD-BPD is rarely straight. You might try five medications before finding what works. You might need combinations that seem unusual. You might need doses outside the typical range.

This isn't failure – it's personalization. Your brain is unique. Your symptoms are unique. Your medication needs are unique.

Some people find their perfect combination quickly. Others take years. Some need multiple medications. Others do well on just one. Some need medication forever. Others use it as a bridge while building skills.

What matters is finding what works for YOUR brain. Not what worked for someone else with BPD. Not what the textbook says about ADHD. What helps YOU function better, feel more stable, and build the life you want.

Chapter 7: Beyond DBT - CBT, Schema Therapy, and Integrated Approaches

The email that changed Marcus's life came on a Tuesday. "I think we need to try something different," his therapist had written. After two years of DBT, Marcus had made progress – he self-harmed less, his relationships were slightly more stable. But something fundamental hadn't shifted. He still felt broken at his core, still couldn't maintain focus long enough to build anything meaningful, still felt like he was performing life rather than living it.

"DBT gave me tools to manage the storms," Marcus explained in his first session with a new therapist who specialized in integrated treatment. "But I'm tired of storm management. I want to understand why I'm a hurricane magnet in the first place."

Over the next year, Marcus engaged in what his therapist called an "integrated approach" – schema therapy to address his core beliefs, CBT to rebuild executive function, EMDR to process trauma, all while maintaining his DBT skills. It wasn't about choosing one therapy over another. It was about using different approaches for different aspects of his dual diagnosis.

"Turns out," Marcus said later, "I didn't need THE answer. I needed multiple answers for my multiple challenges."

Why One Therapy Isn't Enough

If you've been in DBT for a while, you might have noticed something: it's incredible for managing symptoms but doesn't always address root causes. DBT teaches you how to survive the storm. But what about preventing storms? What about rebuilding after storms? What about understanding why you're prone to storms in the first place?

With ADHD-BPD, you're dealing with:

- Neurobiological differences (ADHD)
- Emotional dysregulation (both)
- Trauma (common in both)
- Cognitive distortions (both)
- Identity disturbance (BPD)
- Executive dysfunction (ADHD)
- Core beliefs about defectiveness (both)

No single therapy addresses all of this. DBT is essential but not sufficient. You need a therapeutic toolkit as complex as your challenges.

CBT for Executive Function and Organization

Cognitive Behavioral Therapy for ADHD looks different from traditional CBT. It's less about changing thoughts and more about building systems to compensate for executive dysfunction. When you add BPD to the mix, it needs even more adaptation.

Traditional CBT Says: "Identify the negative thought, challenge it, replace it."

ADHD-CBT Says: "Your thoughts are fine, but your brain can't organize them. Let's build external structures."

ADHD-BPD-CBT Says: "You have both thinking errors AND organizational problems, and they make each other worse. Let's address both while acknowledging your emotional intensity."

Here's how it works in practice:

Time Management Systems: Standard planners assume consistent executive function. You need what I call "crisis-proof planning":

- Buffer time for emotional storms (30% more than you think)
- Backup plans for when you can't function

- Flexible deadlines where possible
- Visual systems (colors, not just words)
- Multiple reminder systems (phone, sticky notes, accountability buddy)

Task Initiation Strategies: You're not just procrastinating – your brain literally can't start. Add emotional overwhelm, and tasks become impossible. CBT helps build "launch sequences":

- Break tasks into stupidly small steps
- Create physical starting rituals
- Use body doubling (working alongside someone)
- Gamify boring tasks
- Tie tasks to values when motivation fails

Cognitive Restructuring with Emotional Validation: Your thoughts might be distorted, but your emotions are real. ADHD-BPD-CBT acknowledges both:

- "I'm a complete failure" becomes "I'm struggling with executive dysfunction AND it feels devastating"
- "Everyone will abandon me" becomes "My ADHD mistakes trigger real abandonment fears"
- "I can't do anything right" becomes "My brain works differently AND that's really hard"

Problem-Solving with Emotional Regulation: Standard problem-solving assumes emotional stability. Yours needs built-in regulation:

1. Recognize problem AND emotional state
2. Regulate enough to think (TIPP if needed)
3. Generate solutions (even bad ones)

4. Pick good-enough solution (not perfect)
5. Try it with self-compassion
6. Learn without shame spiraling

Schema Therapy: Rewriting Your Origin Story

Schema therapy is showing remarkable results for BPD – one study found 94% of participants no longer met BPD criteria after treatment. When you add ADHD to the picture, schema therapy becomes even more relevant because both conditions create similar negative core beliefs.

Schemas are deep beliefs about yourself and the world, formed in childhood. With ADHD-BPD, you likely have some combination of:

Defectiveness/Shame: "I'm inherently flawed, and if people really knew me, they'd reject me." ADHD adds: "I can't even do basic things others do easily." BPD adds: "My emotions are too much for anyone to handle."

Abandonment/Instability: "Everyone I love will leave me." ADHD adds: "They'll leave because I'm too much work." BPD adds: "I'll do anything to prevent them leaving."

Failure: "I'm incompetent and will fail at everything." ADHD adds: "I have proof – look at all my unfinished projects." BPD adds: "And failure means I'm worthless as a person."

Insufficient Self-Control: "I can't control myself like others can." ADHD adds: "My brain won't cooperate." BPD adds: "My emotions overwhelm everything."

Schema therapy doesn't just identify these beliefs – it heals them through:

Limited Reparenting: Your therapist provides what you needed but didn't get in childhood – consistent validation, stable attachment, accurate mirroring. For ADHD-BPD, this might mean:

- Celebrating small wins your parents overlooked
- Staying consistent despite your emotional storms
- Seeing your sensitivity as a strength
- Acknowledging your different brain without judgment

Experiential Techniques: Not just talking about schemas but feeling and changing them:

- Chair work where you dialogue with different parts
- Imagery rescripting where you revisit childhood memories
- Letter writing to younger you or to parents
- Role-playing new ways of being

Mode Work: Schema therapy recognizes you have different "modes" or states. With ADHD-BPD, you might have:

- Vulnerable child (scared, abandoned)
- Angry/impulsive child (ADHD impulsivity meets BPD rage)
- Detached protector (spacing out to avoid pain)
- Punitive parent (internalized criticism)
- Healthy adult (developing slowly)

The goal isn't eliminating modes but helping the healthy adult care for the vulnerable parts and manage the protective parts.

EMDR for the Trauma Layer

Here's a statistic that should be talked about more: 57% of people with BPD also have PTSD. Add ADHD, and trauma rates are even higher. Sometimes what looks like ADHD is trauma. Sometimes what looks like BPD is trauma. Sometimes trauma makes both conditions worse.

EMDR (Eye Movement Desensitization and Reprocessing) can help, but it needs adaptation for ADHD-BPD:

Preparation Phase Modifications:

- Longer preparation because emotional dysregulation makes processing intense
- Extra focus on dual awareness (noticing present while processing past)
- More stabilization exercises
- Clear plans for managing post-session dysregulation

Processing Adaptations:

- Shorter processing sets (15-20 seconds vs 30+)
- More frequent check-ins
- Movement alternatives for hyperactive bodies (tapping, walking)
- Written tracking because working memory struggles

Targets Specific to ADHD-BPD:

- First memories of being "too much"
- Shame experiences around ADHD failures
- Abandonment experiences
- Times when emotional intensity caused problems
- Memories of not being believed or validated

Integration Challenges:

- ADHD makes it harder to maintain dual awareness
- BPD emotional intensity can overwhelm processing
- Both conditions affect memory consolidation
- Dissociation is common with both

But when it works, EMDR can:

- Reduce emotional charge of trigger memories
- Decrease flashbacks and intrusive thoughts
- Improve self-concept
- Reduce shame and self-blame
- Clear trauma that maintains both conditions

The Power of Integrated Treatment

The most effective approach for ADHD-BPD isn't choosing one therapy – it's strategic integration. Think of it like building a house:

Foundation: Stabilization and safety (DBT skills, medication management) **Framework**: Cognitive and behavioral structure (CBT for ADHD) **Wiring**: Trauma processing (EMDR or trauma-focused therapy) **Interior Design**: Core belief work (Schema therapy) **Maintenance**: Ongoing support and skill reinforcement

Different phases might emphasize different approaches:

Crisis Phase: Heavy DBT, medication stabilization, safety planning **Stabilization Phase**: DBT plus CBT for structure, beginning trauma work **Growth Phase**: Schema therapy, deeper trauma processing, identity work **Integration Phase**: Combining all approaches, generalizing skills **Maintenance Phase**: Periodic boosters, continued medication management

Building Your Treatment Team

Integrated treatment often requires multiple providers. Your team might include:

Primary Therapist: Ideally trained in multiple modalities or willing to coordinate. They're your main support and help integrate different approaches.

Psychiatrist: Manages medication and monitors stability. Should communicate with therapist regularly.

Specialist Therapists: Maybe you see someone for EMDR, someone else for DBT group. That's okay if everyone communicates.

ADHD Coach: Helps with practical executive function challenges therapy doesn't address.

Peer Support: Others with dual diagnosis who get it.

Body-Based Practitioner: Yoga therapist, somatic experiencing practitioner, massage therapist – trauma lives in the body.

Coordination is crucial. Everyone needs to know:

- Current medications and changes
- Which therapy phase you're in
- Recent triggers or crises
- What approaches are helping
- Your current goals and challenges

Questions to Ask Potential Therapists

Finding therapists who can work integratively with ADHD-BPD requires good interviewing:

Training Questions:

- "What modalities are you trained in?"
- "How do you integrate different approaches?"
- "What's your experience with ADHD and BPD together?"
- "Are you willing to coordinate with other providers?"

Approach Questions:

- "How do you balance symptom management with deeper work?"
- "When would you use DBT vs CBT vs other approaches?"
- "How do you handle executive dysfunction in therapy?"
- "What's your approach to trauma with emotional dysregulation?"

Practical Questions:

- "How do you handle missed sessions due to executive dysfunction?"
- "Can you provide session recordings for ADHD memory issues?"
- "What's your between-session contact policy?"
- "How do you adapt homework for executive dysfunction?"

Red Flags:

- "I only use one approach for everything"
- "ADHD isn't real/relevant to therapy"
- "BPD has to be completely stable before addressing anything else"
- "Medication is cheating/unnecessary"
- "You're too complex for outpatient treatment"

Making Different Therapies Work Together

The challenge with multiple therapeutic approaches is making them synergistic rather than confusing. Here's how:

Create a Master Treatment Plan: Write down (because you'll forget):

- Which therapy addresses which symptoms

- Current focus in each therapy
- How approaches complement each other
- What to work on where

Use a Common Language: Different therapies use different terms for similar concepts:

- DBT "wise mind" = CBT "balanced thinking" = Schema "healthy adult"
- DBT "emotion mind" = Schema "vulnerable child"
- EMDR "resources" = DBT "skills"

Track What Works Where: Notice which approach helps with which challenge:

- DBT for emotional crises
- CBT for daily functioning
- Schema for relationship patterns
- EMDR for specific triggers

Integrate Skills Across Contexts: Use DBT skills during EMDR. Apply CBT organization to schema work. Bring schema insights to DBT group.

The Hope of Comprehensive Healing

Here's what integrated treatment offers that single-modality therapy doesn't: the possibility of actual healing, not just symptom management.

DBT keeps you alive and stable. CBT helps you function. Schema therapy heals core wounds. EMDR clears trauma. Together, they don't just help you survive with ADHD-BPD – they help you thrive.

You might always have a sensitive nervous system. You might always need more structure than others. But with comprehensive treatment, you can:

- Understand your patterns
- Heal your core wounds
- Build sustainable systems
- Process your trauma
- Develop genuine self-compassion
- Create meaningful relationships
- Pursue authentic goals

The journey is longer and more complex than single-diagnosis treatment. But you're not a single-diagnosis person. You deserve treatment as multifaceted as you are.

Chapter 8: Crisis Planning When You Have Two Ticking Clocks

The text came at 2 AM: "I'm safe now. But I almost wasn't."

Rachel had sent it to her crisis buddy after spending three hours on her bathroom floor, fighting the strongest self-harm urge she'd had in months. What triggered it? A combination that would sound ridiculous to anyone without ADHD-BPD: She'd forgotten an important deadline (ADHD), which made her feel like a failure (BPD), which triggered shame about being "broken" (both), which activated self-harm urges (BPD), which felt impossible to resist because her executive function was shot (ADHD).

"The thing is," Rachel explained in therapy the next week, "I had all my DBT skills. I knew what to do. But my ADHD brain couldn't access them, and my BPD brain was screaming so loud I couldn't think. It was like being in a burning building with a fire extinguisher I couldn't remember how to use."

That session, Rachel and her therapist created what they called a "dual crisis plan" – one that accounted for both the emotional intensity of BPD and the executive dysfunction of ADHD. It wasn't just about having skills. It was about making those skills accessible when both conditions were firing at once.

Understanding Your Unique Crisis Pattern

Crisis with ADHD-BPD doesn't follow the textbook patterns. It's not just emotional dysregulation or just impulsive behavior. It's a specific sequence where each condition amplifies the other:

The ADHD-BPD Crisis Cascade:

1. ADHD mistake/failure/overwhelm occurs

2. BPD shame/abandonment/emptiness triggers
3. Emotional dysregulation floods system
4. Executive function completely shuts down
5. Can't access coping skills
6. Impulsivity increases (both conditions)
7. Acting on urges feels like only option
8. Crisis behavior occurs
9. Shame spiral intensifies everything
10. Recovery takes longer due to both conditions

Understanding your personal cascade helps predict and interrupt it. Maybe yours starts with rejection sensitivity (ADHD) triggering abandonment panic (BPD). Or sensory overwhelm (ADHD) triggering dissociation (BPD). Or identity confusion (BPD) worsened by inconsistent functioning (ADHD).

Map your pattern:

- What typically starts the cascade?
- Where does ADHD hand off to BPD (or vice versa)?
- What makes it worse?
- Where are potential interruption points?
- What has helped before (even slightly)?

The TIPP Skills Turbocharged

Standard TIPP skills help with BPD crisis, but need major amplification for ADHD-BPD crisis:

Temperature - Make It Shocking: Regular: Hold ice cubes ADHD-BPD Version: Full cold shower, head in freezer, ice pack on neck

AND wrists simultaneously. Your nervous system needs a full reset, not a gentle suggestion.

Intense Exercise - But Different: Regular: 20 minutes of cardio ADHD-BPD Version: 30 seconds of maximum intensity (burpees, sprinting in place), rest 30 seconds, repeat 5 times. Your attention span is shot during crisis – work with it.

Paced Breathing - With Movement: Regular: Sit and breathe slowly ADHD-BPD Version: Walk and breathe to your steps. Four steps in, hold four steps, four steps out. Your body needs to move while your breath slows.

Progressive Muscle Relaxation - Speed Version: Regular: Slowly tense and release each muscle ADHD-BPD Version: Tense everything at once for 5 seconds, then complete release. Repeat 3 times. Quick, effective, doesn't require sustained focus.

Building Your Crisis Kit

Standard crisis kits assume you'll remember what's in them and how to use items. ADHD-BPD crisis kits need to be foolproof:

The Container: Bright red box labeled "CRISIS" in huge letters. Not subtle. When you're dissociating, you need obvious.

Contents with Instructions:

Ice pack with tag: "PUT ON NECK NOW"

Sour candy with note: "EAT THREE"

Essential oil with instruction: "SMELL DEEPLY 5 TIMES"

Stress ball with reminder: "SQUEEZE HARD 20 TIMES"

Photos with labels: "YOU ARE LOVED" "THIS WILL PASS"

Playlist card: "PRESS PLAY ON CRISIS PLAYLIST"

Index cards with one skill per card:

- Card 1: "SPLASH COLD WATER ON FACE"
- Card 2: "DO 20 JUMPING JACKS"
- Card 3: "CALL CRISIS BUDDY"
- Card 4: "TAKE PRN MEDICATION"

Multiple Kits: Have them everywhere – car, bedroom, bathroom, work. Executive dysfunction means you won't go looking for it.

Safety Planning for Self-Harm and Suicidal Thoughts

Let's be real: many people with BPD experience self-harm urges and suicidal ideation. Add ADHD impulsivity, and the risk increases. A good safety plan acknowledges both conditions:

Means Restriction with ADHD Adaptations:

- Remove means when stable, not during crisis (you won't remember during crisis)
- Use time-delay safes for medications
- Give extra meds to trusted person
- Remove items impulsively grabbed (not just planned means)
- Account for creative ADHD problem-solving in crisis

Warning Signs - Dual Diagnosis Version:

- ADHD signs: Hyperfocus on negative thoughts, inability to start tasks, time blindness increasing
- BPD signs: Emptiness increasing, relationship fears spiking, identity confusion worsening
- Combination signs: Mistakes triggering shame spirals, rejection creating paralysis

Coping Strategies Ladder: Start with least intensive, climb if needed:

1. Sensory grounding (name 5 things you see)
2. Physical reset (cold water, jumping jacks)
3. Distraction (specific activity for 20 minutes)
4. Reach out (text crisis buddy)
5. Use skills (TIPP, DBT skills)
6. Take PRN medication
7. Call therapist/warmline
8. Go to safe person
9. Call crisis line
10. Go to emergency room

The "If I Can Just..." Contract: During crisis, agree to:

- Wait 24 hours before acting on urges
- Tell one person how you're feeling
- Try three skills from your list
- Take medication if prescribed
- Sleep on it (literally, try to sleep)

ADHD Impulsivity Meeting BPD Desperation

The combination of ADHD impulsivity and BPD emotional desperation creates unique crisis risks:

The "Fuck It" Moment: You know that moment when executive function collapses, emotional pain peaks, and you just think "fuck it" and act? That's both conditions creating a perfect storm. Plan for it:

- Recognize it as a neurological event, not a character flaw
- Have a "fuck it" protocol (specific action to take instead)

- Create maximum barriers to harmful impulsive acts
- Have someone to call who understands this specific moment

The Time Blindness Factor: ADHD makes you forget that feelings pass. BPD makes feelings feel eternal. Together, crisis feels permanent. Counter this:

- Set timers: "Check in with yourself in 20 minutes"
- Look at photos from good times (they existed)
- Read letters from future self (written when stable)
- Use apps that show mood patterns over time

The Rejection Sensitivity Spiral: RSD (ADHD) plus abandonment fears (BPD) can create instant crisis from small rejections:

- Have a "rejection protocol" ready
- Fact-check abandonment thoughts
- 24-hour rule before acting on relationship fears
- Pre-written self-compassion scripts

Emergency Resources Tailored for You

Standard crisis resources might not work well with ADHD-BPD:

Crisis Lines That Get It:

- National Suicide Prevention Lifeline: 988
- Crisis Text Line: Text HOME to 741741
- NAMI Helpline: 1-800-950-NAMI (6264)
- The Trevor Project (LGBTQ+): 1-866-488-7386

But also:

- Have numbers saved with labels like "CALL WHEN SUICIDAL"

- Use text lines if phone calls are too much
- Try warm lines for non-crisis support
- Use apps like Sanvello or Youper for immediate support

When to Go to the ER:
- You have a specific plan and means
- You can't stop yourself from acting
- You've already hurt yourself significantly
- You're experiencing psychosis or severe dissociation
- Your support system agrees you need immediate help

ER Survival Kit: If you go, bring:
- List of medications (you won't remember)
- Therapist contact info
- Comfort items (soft fabric, fidget toy)
- Phone charger
- Snacks (hospital waits + ADHD + emotional stress = disaster)
- Someone who can advocate for you

Creating Your Personal Crisis Protocol

Your crisis plan needs to be ADHD-friendly (simple, visual, accessible) and BPD-informed (validating, comprehensive, relationship-inclusive):

The One-Page Version (laminated, everywhere):

CRISIS PROTOCOL

1. STOP
- Stop what you're doing

- Take 3 deep breaths
- Touch your crisis bracelet

2. SAFE

- Am I safe right now? If no → call 988
- Can I stay safe for 20 minutes? If no → call crisis buddy
- Do I need medication? If yes → take it

3. SHOCK

- Cold water on face
- Or ice on neck
- Or 30 seconds intense exercise

4. SUPPORT

- Text crisis buddy: "I'm struggling"
- Or call warmline
- Or go to safe person

5. SKILL

- Try one DBT skill
- For 10 minutes only
- Good enough is good enough

6. SURVIVE

- You only have to survive this moment
- Then the next moment
- That's all

The Crisis Buddy System

Having a crisis buddy who understands ADHD-BPD is invaluable. This person:

- Knows your patterns
- Can remind you of skills when you forget
- Provides body doubling during crisis
- Helps with executive function when it's gone
- Validates emotions while encouraging safety

Crisis Buddy Agreement includes:

- When to call (specific signs, not just "crisis")
- What help looks like (listening, reminding, coming over)
- Boundaries (they're support, not a therapist)
- Backup plan (who to call if they're unavailable)
- Check-in schedule (daily during hard times)

Post-Crisis Recovery

Recovery from crisis takes longer with ADHD-BPD. Both conditions affect your ability to bounce back:

The Shame Hangover Protocol:

- Acknowledge you survived something hard
- Avoid immediate analysis (your cognition is impaired)
- Do basic self-care (shower, eat, sleep)
- Contact therapist within 24 hours
- Process only when regulated

The Executive Function Rebuild:

- Start with tiny tasks (brush teeth)

- Use body doubling for basic functions
- Lower all expectations temporarily
- Ask for help with urgent tasks
- Slowly increase demands over days

The Emotional Reset:

- Expect vulnerability for 48-72 hours
- Use preventive DBT skills
- Avoid major decisions
- Increase check-ins with support
- Be boring (routine, predictable, safe)

Crisis Doesn't Define You

Having a crisis plan isn't admitting defeat – it's accepting reality and preparing for it. Everyone with ADHD-BPD will face crisis moments. The difference between those who thrive and those who struggle isn't avoiding crisis altogether – it's having a plan that actually works when both conditions are firing.

Your crisis plan is like insurance: you hope not to need it, but you're damn glad it's there when you do. It's not about being dramatic or attention-seeking or any of the other bullshit people might have told you. It's about acknowledging that your brain faces unique challenges and deserves unique support.

Every crisis you survive makes you stronger. Every time you use your plan instead of acting on impulse, you're rewiring your brain. Every moment you choose safety despite the chaos, you're proving that both conditions can be managed.

Section III: Daily Life Strategies
Practical Management for Real Life

Chapter 9: Relationships - When Attachment Meets Attention

Love came easy for Emma. It always had. The falling part, anyway. Within three dates, she'd be planning their future, memorizing their coffee order, reshaping her entire personality to match what she thought they wanted. By month two, the cracks would show. She'd forget important conversations (ADHD), then panic that forgetting meant she didn't care (BPD). She'd interrupt constantly during arguments (ADHD), then interpret their frustration as abandonment (BPD). By month three, she'd either cling so tightly they'd run, or she'd blow everything up preemptively to avoid the rejection she was certain was coming.

"I don't understand," she told her therapist after her latest breakup. "I love harder than anyone I know. I give everything. Why does it always fall apart?"

Her therapist leaned forward. "What if loving hard isn't the same as loving well? What if your brain needs different relationship strategies than the ones you've been using?"

That conversation changed everything. Emma spent the next year learning how ADHD and BPD specifically affected her relationships, and more importantly, what to do about it. By the time she met her current partner, she had a toolkit. Not perfect solutions, but real strategies for managing the intersection of attachment terror and attention deficits.

The Perfect Storm of Connection Difficulties

Relationships with ADHD-BPD aren't just challenging – they're challenging in specific, predictable ways. Understanding these patterns is the first step to changing them.

The ADHD contribution:
- Forgetting important dates, conversations, or agreements
- Interrupting during emotional discussions
- Getting distracted during quality time
- Inconsistent communication patterns
- Time blindness affecting reliability
- Hyperfocus on new relationships, neglect of established ones
- Missing social cues and nonverbal communication

The BPD contribution:
- Fear of abandonment triggering clingy or pushing behaviors
- Idealization followed by devaluation
- Emotional reactions disproportionate to triggers
- Identity shifting to match partners
- Testing behaviors to confirm love
- Inability to hold onto positive memories during conflict
- Black-and-white thinking about relationship status

The deadly combination: When these overlap, you get unique patterns like:

- Forgetting something important (ADHD) → catastrophizing about what it means (BPD) → panic response that damages relationship → confirmation that you ruin everything
- Hyperfocusing on a new person (ADHD) → instant attachment (BPD) → overwhelming intensity that scares them away → abandonment confirmation

- Missing subtle relationship issues (ADHD) → sudden realization things are wrong (BPD) → extreme response to save or end relationship → chaos and confusion

Communication Frameworks That Actually Work

Standard communication advice assumes neurotypical processing. "Just listen actively." Sure, except your ADHD brain is ping-ponging between seventeen thoughts while your BPD brain is scanning for rejection. You need adapted frameworks.

DEAR MAN for the Dual Diagnosis Brain:

Describe - But write it down first. Your emotional brain will hijack your words if you wing it. Script: "When X happened, I observed Y."

Express - Own both conditions' impact. "My rejection sensitivity is making this feel huge, and my ADHD means I might have missed something. Here's how I'm experiencing this..."

Assert - State needs clearly, once. ADHD makes you repeat. BPD makes you over-explain. Say it once, clearly.

Reinforce - Focus on mutual benefit. "This will help both of us by..."

Mindful - Stay on topic despite mental ping-pong. Have your script visible. When you drift, return to script.

Appear Confident - Even though you feel like you're dying inside. Stand up straight, make eye contact, speak steadily.

Negotiate - Be willing to compromise but know your bottom line in advance. Write down acceptable alternatives before the conversation.

The Three-Touch Rule for Important Conversations:

1. First mention: Plant the seed. "We need to talk about X sometime soon."

2. Second mention: Schedule it. "Can we talk about X tomorrow at 7?"

3. Third mention: The actual conversation, with both parties prepared

This gives ADHD brains time to process and BPD brains time to regulate.

Managing the Rejection Sensitivity Double Whammy

Rejection Sensitive Dysphoria (ADHD) plus abandonment fears (BPD) creates a special kind of hell. Perceived rejection – even imagined rejection – can trigger a full-system meltdown.

The Rejection Reality Check Protocol:

1. **Notice the trigger**: "They didn't text back immediately"

2. **Label the response**: "RSD and abandonment fear are activating"

3. **Check the facts**: "They're at work. This is normal."

4. **Use opposite action**: Instead of panic texting, do something self-soothing

5. **Reconnect when calm**: "Hey, hope your day's going well"

Creating Rejection Resilience:

- Build a "rejection resume" of times you survived rejection

- Practice small rejections (ask for things likely to be denied)

- Develop rejection rituals (specific self-care after rejection)

- Create rejection buddies (people who understand the intensity)

- Plan rejection responses in advance (if X happens, I'll do Y)

The 24-Hour Rule: When you feel rejected, wait 24 hours before acting on it. No breakup texts, no confrontations, no major decisions. Your brain needs time to sort real from perceived rejection.

Boundary Setting When Your Brain Resists Boundaries

Boundaries are hard for everyone, but ADHD-BPD makes them exponentially harder. ADHD forgets boundaries exist. BPD fears boundaries will cause abandonment. Together, they create chaotic boundary patterns.

The Boundary Gradient System: Instead of hard boundaries that you'll impulsively break or anxiously abandon, create gradient boundaries:

Level 1: Preferences ("I prefer when you...") Level 2: Requests ("I need you to...") Level 3: Requirements ("I cannot continue if...") Level 4: Deal-breakers ("This relationship cannot work with...")

Start at Level 1. Only escalate if needed. This gives your brain adjustment time and reduces all-or-nothing thinking.

Boundary Scripts for Common Situations:

When you need space but fear abandonment: "I need some alone time to recharge. This isn't about you or us – it's about my brain needing quiet. I love you and I'll be back in [specific time]."

When ADHD made you overcommit: "I realized I can't actually do X. My brain was too optimistic about time/energy. Can we find an alternative that works for both of us?"

When emotional intensity overwhelms others: "I'm having a big emotion that's not proportional to the situation. I need [specific thing] right now. You don't need to fix it."

Family Dynamics and Education

Family relationships carry extra weight with ADHD-BPD. These are often the people who've witnessed your struggles longest, may have contributed to them, and might have their own neurodivergence.

Educating Family Without Overwhelming:

- Share one article or video at a time, not a library
- Focus on specific behaviors, not general diagnosis
- Use "I" statements: "My brain works like this..."
- Provide concrete examples from shared experiences
- Offer specific ways they can help

The Family Meeting Framework: Monthly family meetings can prevent crisis-driven communication:

1. Check-in round (everyone shares their current state)
2. Appreciation round (acknowledge positive things)
3. Problem-solving (one issue at a time)
4. Planning (upcoming events, needs)
5. Close with connection (game, meal, activity)

Dealing with Invalidating Family: Some families can't or won't understand. Strategies for managing:

- Information diet (share less about struggles)
- Gray rock technique (be boring during conflict)
- Strategic distance (less contact during vulnerable times)
- Chosen family development (build supportive relationships elsewhere)
- Therapy for family trauma (your healing isn't dependent on their change)

Building and Maintaining Friendships

Friendships with ADHD-BPD often follow a pattern: intense initial connection, overwhelming closeness, forgotten maintenance, perceived rejection, dramatic ending. Breaking this pattern requires intentional strategies.

The Friendship Maintenance System:

- Set recurring reminders to check in with friends
- Create a "friendship spreadsheet" tracking last contact
- Develop friendship rituals (weekly text, monthly coffee)
- Use voice messages when executive function is low
- Be honest about your challenges: "I'm terrible at keeping in touch but I care about you"

Managing Friendship Intensity:

- Resist the urge to become instant best friends
- Spread emotional needs across multiple friendships
- Have different friends for different needs
- Practice sharing yourself in portions, not all at once
- Allow friendships to develop slowly

The Friendship Repair Conversation: "I realize I've been [specific behavior]. My ADHD/emotional stuff got in the way. You matter to me and I want to do better. Can we talk about what you need from me as a friend?"

Romantic Relationships That Survive and Thrive

Romantic relationships trigger both conditions maximally. The intensity, the stakes, the intimacy – it all activates your symptoms. But healthy romantic relationships are absolutely possible.

Early Dating Adaptations:

- Date slowly (even though your brain wants to merge immediately)
- Keep your routine (don't abandon your life for new person)

- Tell friends about red flags you're ignoring
- Set date limits (two per week maximum initially)
- Continue therapy throughout early dating
- Don't move in together impulsively

Living Together Strategies:

- Separate spaces for when you need distance
- Visual schedules for household tasks
- Regular relationship check-ins
- Clear communication about emotional states
- Flexibility around different organizational needs
- Acceptance that you'll do things differently

The Daily Emotional Weather Report: Each partner shares their emotional/cognitive state each morning:

- Emotional baseline (1-10)
- Executive function capacity (high/medium/low)
- Specific triggers to avoid
- Support needs for the day
- Appreciation for partner

This prevents misinterpretation and allows for daily adjustment.

Sex and Intimacy Considerations

Both conditions affect sexual and intimate relationships in complex ways:

ADHD factors:

- Distraction during sex

- Sensory sensitivities
- Medication effects on libido
- Hyperfocus on sex or complete forgetfulness
- Need for novelty and stimulation

BPD factors:

- Sex as validation or abandonment prevention
- Identity confusion affecting sexual preferences
- Emotional dysregulation during intimacy
- Fear of vulnerability
- Intensity overwhelming partners

Healthy Intimacy Strategies:

- Communicate needs and boundaries outside the bedroom
- Address distraction compassionately ("Let's pause and reconnect")
- Separate sex from emotional regulation
- Build non-sexual intimacy too
- Be honest about medication effects
- Create sensory-friendly intimate environments

The Support Network Approach

No one person can meet all your relational needs, especially with ADHD-BPD. Building a support network reduces pressure on individual relationships:

Your Network Might Include:

- Romantic partner(s) for intimacy and companionship

- Best friend(s) for emotional processing
- Activity friends for dopamine and fun
- Crisis buddy for emergency support
- Therapy for professional support
- Support group for peer understanding
- Family (chosen or biological) for roots
- Colleagues for professional connection
- Mentors for guidance

Each relationship has different expectations and boundaries. Not everyone needs to understand everything about you.

Relationships Are Possible and Worth It

Here's what nobody tells you about relationships with ADHD-BPD: they can be extraordinarily rich. Your sensitivity means you love deeply. Your intensity means you're fully present. Your challenges mean you develop incredible communication skills and self-awareness.

Yes, relationships require more work for you. Yes, you'll make mistakes. Yes, some people won't be able to handle your intensity. But the right people – the ones who see you, understand you, and choose you anyway – they're out there.

The goal isn't to have neurotypical relationships. It's to have healthy relationships that work with your neurodiversity. That means different strategies, more communication, greater flexibility, and lots of compassion – for yourself and others.

Every relationship skill you develop, every pattern you break, every healthy connection you maintain is proof that ADHD-BPD doesn't doom you to isolation. You're capable of profound connection. You just need the right tools and the right people.

Chapter 10: Emotional Storms and Executive Function

Michael stared at his to-do list, tears streaming down his face. Not because the list was overwhelming (though it was), but because his partner had used a "tone" at breakfast. Now his entire nervous system was in chaos, his thoughts were scattered like leaves in a hurricane, and the simple task of answering emails felt as impossible as climbing Everest in flip-flops.

"This is ridiculous," he muttered, knowing that berating himself would make it worse but unable to stop. The ADHD made it impossible to prioritize what needed doing. The BPD made everything feel urgently catastrophic. Together, they created a perfect storm where he couldn't think OR feel his way forward.

Three hours later, he'd accomplished nothing except scrolling through his phone, starting and abandoning six different tasks, and sending his partner seventeen texts analyzing their breakfast interaction. The day was shot, which would create tomorrow's crisis, which would trigger tomorrow's emotional storm.

Sound familiar? The intersection of emotional dysregulation and executive dysfunction creates a unique kind of paralysis. But here's what Michael learned: you can't think your way out of an emotional storm, and you can't feel your way through executive dysfunction. You need strategies that address both simultaneously.

When Emotions Hijack Your Brain's CEO

Executive function is like your brain's CEO – planning, organizing, prioritizing, executing. Emotional dysregulation is like a hostile takeover where the board of directors (your emotions) fires the CEO and runs around making impulsive decisions. With ADHD-BPD, you've got a weak CEO and a very aggressive board.

Here's what happens during an emotional hijacking:

- **Working memory evaporates**: You literally can't remember what you were doing
- **Prioritization becomes impossible**: Everything feels equally urgent/impossible
- **Time awareness disappears**: Five minutes or five hours, who knows?
- **Decision-making short-circuits**: Every choice feels wrong
- **Task initiation freezes**: You can't start anything
- **Cognitive flexibility dies**: You can't shift strategies or perspectives

Traditional productivity advice ("Just break it into smaller steps!") assumes your CEO is still in the building. Yours has left the country.

The Emotion-Task Matrix

Instead of treating emotions and tasks as separate, map them together:

High Emotion + High Executive Function Needed = STOP Don't attempt complex tasks while dysregulated. You'll make mistakes that create more problems.

High Emotion + Low Executive Function Needed = MAYBE Simple, routine tasks might be possible. Folding laundry, yes. Taxes, no.

Low Emotion + High Executive Function Needed = GO This is your window for complex tasks. Guard it fiercely.

Low Emotion + Low Executive Function Needed = RESTORE Use calm periods for self-care and preparation, not just mindless scrolling.

Body Doubling and Co-Regulation Magic

Body doubling – working alongside someone else – addresses both ADHD and BPD needs simultaneously. It provides:

- External structure for ADHD chaos
- Social connection for BPD attachment needs
- Accountability without judgment
- Co-regulation of emotional states
- Modeling of task completion

Virtual Body Doubling Options:

- FocusMate for scheduled work sessions
- Discord servers for 24/7 company
- Zoom rooms with friends
- YouTube "Study with Me" videos
- Twitch streams of people working

In-Person Body Doubling:

- Coffee shop working
- Library presence
- Co-working spaces
- Parallel play with partners
- Task parties with friends

The key: the other person doesn't have to help or even talk. Their presence alone regulates your nervous system and improves focus.

Task Management During Emotional Episodes

When emotions are high, traditional task management fails. You need emergency protocols:

The Emotional Day Triage System:

1. **Accept reduced capacity**: You're operating at 30%, not 100%
2. **Identify one must-do**: What will cause the most damage if undone?
3. **Lower the bar to the floor**: Good enough is the goal
4. **Use timers, not goals**: "Work for 10 minutes" not "Finish project"
5. **Build in recovery time**: Emotional storms are exhausting

The Task Bundling Method: Bundle tasks by emotional state rather than category:

- Angry energy tasks: Cleaning, organizing, physical filing
- Sad energy tasks: Gentle emails, routine data entry
- Anxious energy tasks: List-making, planning, researching
- Numb energy tasks: Copying, backing up files, mindless sorting

The Minimum Viable Day: Define the absolute minimum for a day to "count":

- Fed yourself something
- Took medication
- Communicated with one person
- Did one productive thing (tiny counts)
- Practiced one coping skill

Some days, minimum viable is maximum possible. That's okay.

The Modified Pomodoro for Emotional Brains

Standard Pomodoro: 25 minutes work, 5 minute break ADHD-BPD Pomodoro: Flexible based on state

High Emotion Days:

- 10 minutes work
- 5 minutes emotion check
- 10 minutes work
- 10 minutes regulation break

Medium Emotion Days:

- 15 minutes work
- 3 minutes movement
- 15 minutes work
- 7 minutes full break

Low Emotion Days:

- 20-45 minutes work (ride the wave)
- 5-10 minutes break
- Repeat while it lasts

The key: Adjust based on your actual state, not what you think you "should" handle.

Creating Structure That Bends Without Breaking

Rigid structure fails with ADHD-BPD because you can't maintain it during emotional storms. Flexible structure adapts to your changing states while maintaining some consistency.

The Skeleton Schedule: Instead of hour-by-hour planning, create a loose structure:

- Morning: Self-care and planning

- Late morning: High-focus work (if possible)
- Afternoon: Meetings, calls, interactive tasks
- Late afternoon: Low-focus work
- Evening: Wind down and prep tomorrow

Within each block, flexibility based on emotional state.

The Menu Approach: Instead of a fixed to-do list, create menus:
- High energy/low emotion menu
- Low energy/stable emotion menu
- High emotion/any energy menu
- Crisis mode menu

Choose from the appropriate menu based on your state.

The Safety Net System: Build in catches for when structure fails:
- Weekly review to catch dropped balls
- Partner/friend check-ins for accountability
- Automated systems for crucial tasks
- Backup plans for everything important
- Grace periods built into deadlines

Emotional Check-Ins That Actually Help

Standard emotional check-ins ("How are you feeling?") don't provide actionable information. You need specific data:

The STEMS Check-In:
- **S**omatic: What's happening in my body?
- **T**houghts: What's my mental speed/clarity?
- **E**motions: What feelings are present?

- **M**otivation: What's my capacity for action?
- **S**upport: What do I need right now?

The Traffic Light System:

- Green: Good to go, normal capacity
- Yellow: Proceed with caution, reduced capacity
- Red: Stop, emergency protocol needed

Share your color with support people so they know how to help.

Technology Tools for Dual Support

Apps and tools designed for ADHD or BPD alone might not be enough. You need combination approaches:

For Task Management:

- Todoist or Any.do for flexible task scheduling
- Forest app for focus with visual reward
- Habitica for gamification
- Notion for everything in one place

For Emotional Regulation:

- Daylio for mood tracking
- Sanvello for CBT and coping skills
- Youper for AI emotional support
- Insight Timer for guided meditation

For Both:

- Routinery for routine automation
- Tiimo for visual scheduling
- Empath for combined mood and task tracking

- Mind Doc for comprehensive mental health tracking

The Phone Setup:

- Home screen: Only emergency apps and contacts
- Second screen: Daily tools and supports
- Third screen: Distractions (social media, games)
- Use widgets for quick access to coping tools
- Set focus modes for different emotional states

Working With Your Cycles, Not Against Them

Both ADHD and BPD have cycles – energy, emotion, focus, stability. Fighting these cycles wastes energy. Working with them maximizes function.

Track Your Patterns:

- When is focus best/worst?
- What triggers emotional storms?
- How long do storms typically last?
- What helps recovery?
- Are there monthly/seasonal patterns?

Plan Around Patterns:

- Schedule complex tasks for stable times
- Build buffer time around known triggers
- Plan lighter loads during vulnerable periods
- Use peak times for important work
- Protect recovery time after storms

The Surge and Recover Model: Instead of consistent daily output:

- Surge when capable (ride the hyperfocus)
- Maintain during medium times
- Recover during low times
- Don't shame the cycle

The Integration Practice

The ultimate goal isn't to separate emotions from tasks but to integrate them functionally:

Emotional Task Pairing: Use emotions as fuel for appropriate tasks:

- Anger → Physical organization, cleaning
- Sadness → Creative work, journaling
- Anxiety → Detailed planning, research
- Joy → Social tasks, relationship building
- Numbness → Routine maintenance

The Both/And Approach: "I'm dysregulated AND I need to work" becomes: "How can I work WITH my dysregulation?" "What task matches this emotional state?" "How can I honor both needs?"

Compassionate Productivity:

- Progress over perfection
- Effort counts even without results
- Rest is productive for your nervous system
- Emotional processing IS work
- Surviving difficult days is an achievement

Productivity Looks Different for You

Here's the truth: you might never be traditionally productive. Your output will be inconsistent. Your methods will seem chaotic to others. Your relationship with tasks will always be complicated.

But that doesn't mean you can't achieve things. It means you achieve them differently. In waves rather than steady streams. In bursts rather than marathons. In creative chaos rather than linear progress.

The goal isn't to become neurotypical-productive. It's to become YOU-productive. That means working with your emotional storms rather than against them, supporting your executive function rather than shaming it, and creating systems that flex with your changing states.

Some days you'll accomplish miracles. Some days you'll barely survive. Most days will be somewhere in between. And that's not failure – that's life with ADHD-BPD. The more you accept and work with this reality, the more you can actually accomplish.

Chapter 11: Work, Career, and Finding Your Place

Lisa had been fired again. Or, more accurately, she'd "decided to pursue other opportunities" after her manager suggested it might be best. This was job number twelve in eight years. The pattern was always the same: initial enthusiasm and hyperfocus making her a star employee, then the cracks showing – missed deadlines she'd forgotten about, emotional reactions to feedback, intense conflicts with coworkers she'd idealized then devalued, calling in sick during emotional crises.

"Maybe I'm just not meant to work," she said to her therapist, defeat in her voice. "Maybe I should just accept that I'm too broken for capitalism."

Her therapist considered this. "Or maybe you've been trying to force yourself into neurotypical work structures that will never fit your brain. What if instead of finding the 'right' job, you built the right career for your specific neurology?"

That reframe changed everything. Lisa stopped trying to fit herself into standard boxes and started building a career that worked with her ADHD-BPD brain, not against it.

The Unique Challenges You Face at Work

Workplace challenges with ADHD-BPD aren't just doubled – they're exponentially complicated:

ADHD creates:

- Missed deadlines and forgotten meetings
- Difficulty with boring but necessary tasks
- Interrupting in meetings

- Disorganized workspace and files
- Time blindness affecting punctuality
- Hyperfocus making you forget breaks/lunch

BPD creates:

- Extreme reactions to criticism or feedback
- Splitting on colleagues and supervisors
- Identity confusion about career direction
- Emotional storms affecting attendance
- Fear of abandonment during reviews or changes
- Intense workplace relationships

Together they create:

- Forgetting important tasks then panicking about consequences
- Hyperfocusing on work relationships instead of work
- Emotional dysregulation making ADHD symptoms worse
- Imposter syndrome on steroids
- Burnout cycles from unsustainable intensity
- Job hopping when things get difficult

The Disclosure Dilemma

To tell or not to tell? There's no universal right answer, but there are ways to think it through:

Consider Disclosure If:

- You need specific accommodations
- Your symptoms are visible anyway
- The workplace seems genuinely inclusive

- You have legal protections (ADA in the US)
- You're struggling without support

Consider NOT Disclosing If:

- You can manage without accommodations
- The workplace culture is hostile to mental health
- You're in a probationary period
- You haven't established credibility yet
- You have other ways to get needs met

The Partial Disclosure Strategy: Instead of "I have ADHD and BPD," try:

- "I work best with written instructions"
- "I need quiet space to concentrate"
- "I'm most productive with regular check-ins"
- "I benefit from clear, direct feedback"

You're describing needs, not diagnoses.

Accommodation Strategies That Actually Work

Legal accommodations are your right (in many countries), but knowing what to ask for is crucial:

ADHD Accommodations:

- Written instructions for verbal assignments
- Regular check-ins with supervisors
- Quiet workspace or noise-canceling headphones
- Flexible scheduling for peak focus times
- Break reminders and movement breaks

- Task prioritization assistance

BPD Accommodations:

- Advance notice of changes
- Regular, structured feedback
- Clear communication protocols
- Time to process emotional responses
- Consistent supervisory relationship
- Modified attendance for therapy

Combination Accommodations:

- Work from home options for difficult days
- Recorded meetings for review later
- Extended deadlines with check-in points
- Job coaching or mentorship
- Modified probationary periods
- Gradual increase in responsibilities

The Accommodation Request Template:

"Dear [HR/Supervisor],

I am requesting workplace accommodations under the [ADA/relevant law]. I have medical conditions that affect my concentration and emotional regulation. These conditions are well-managed with treatment, but some accommodations would help me perform at my best.

Specifically, I am requesting:

1. [Specific accommodation]
2. [Specific accommodation]

3. [Specific accommodation]

These accommodations will allow me to [specific benefit to performance]. I'm happy to discuss these further and provide documentation from my healthcare provider.

Thank you for your consideration."

Managing Workplace Relationships

Workplace relationships trigger both conditions intensely. You need strategies for professional boundaries:

The Professional Persona Framework: Create a work version of yourself that's authentic but boundaried:

- Friendly but not friends
- Helpful but not self-sacrificing
- Engaged but not enmeshed
- Professional but not cold

The Relationship Gradient:

- Level 1: Courteous colleagues (most people)
- Level 2: Friendly colleagues (regular interaction)
- Level 3: Work friends (some personal sharing)
- Level 4: Actual friends (happens to work together)

Don't jump to Level 4 with everyone.

Managing Splitting at Work: When you start seeing a colleague as all-good or all-bad:

1. Notice the split happening
2. Write down three neutral facts about them
3. Remind yourself they're complex humans

4. Limit interaction until you're regulated
   5. Seek supervision if needed

The Feedback Protocol: Criticism hits different with RSD and abandonment fears:

   1. Ask for feedback in writing when possible
   2. Take 24 hours to process before responding
   3. Separate professional feedback from personal worth
   4. Ask clarifying questions when calm
   5. Thank them for the feedback (even if it hurt)

Career Planning with Identity Flexibility

Traditional career planning assumes you know who you are and what you want. With ADHD-BPD identity fluctuation, you need different approaches:

The Portfolio Career Model: Instead of one career path, build multiple income streams:

- Part-time employment for stability
- Freelance work for flexibility
- Passion projects for identity
- Skill development for future options

The Cycle Career Model: Acknowledge that your interests cycle:

- Work in tech for two years
- Switch to education for 18 months
- Try nonprofit work
- Return to tech with new perspective
- This isn't failure; it's your pattern

The Mission-Based Model: Find an overarching mission that can be expressed different ways:

- "Helping people" can be healthcare, teaching, social work, tech support
- "Creating beauty" can be design, writing, landscaping, organizing
- "Solving problems" can be engineering, therapy, research, consulting

Values-Based Planning: Since interests change, focus on consistent values:

- Flexibility and autonomy
- Helping others
- Creative expression
- Intellectual stimulation
- Financial security

Find careers that honor these regardless of specific role.

Handling Criticism Without Imploding

Criticism at work can trigger both RSD and abandonment fears, creating intense reactions that can damage your career:

The SPACE Response:

- **S**top: Don't respond immediately
- **P**rocess: What exactly was said?
- **A**ssess: Is this about behavior or identity?
- **C**onsider: What's true, what's not?
- **E**ngage: Respond professionally when calm

Scripts for Difficult Feedback: "Thank you for this feedback. I need some time to process it properly. Can we discuss it further tomorrow?"

"I appreciate you bringing this to my attention. I'm having a strong emotional response, so I'd like to think about it and respond thoughtfully."

"This is hard to hear, but I want to understand. Can you give me specific examples so I can improve?"

The Feedback Reframe: Instead of: "They hate me and I'm getting fired" Try: "They want me to succeed and are helping me improve"

Instead of: "I'm a complete failure" Try: "I have a specific skill to develop"

Creating Your ADHD-BPD Friendly Work Environment

You can't control everything, but you can optimize what you can:

Physical Space:

- Noise management (headphones, white noise)
- Visual calm (minimal clutter, hidden supplies)
- Sensory comfort (fidgets, stress ball, soft fabric)
- Reminder systems (sticky notes, visual cues)
- Crisis kit (medication, snacks, comfort items)

Temporal Structure:

- Block scheduling for different task types
- Protected focus time
- Regular breaks built in
- Buffer time between meetings
- Flexibility for bad days

Social Structure:
- Identify safe colleagues
- Find a work mentor
- Build in alone time
- Create interaction boundaries
- Develop scripts for common situations

Task Management:
- External project management tools
- Visual progress tracking
- Breaking large projects into tiny steps
- Deadline cushions
- Regular check-ins

When Traditional Employment Doesn't Work

Sometimes, despite all accommodations and strategies, traditional employment just doesn't fit. That's not failure – it's information.

Alternative Work Structures:
- Freelancing/consulting
- Part-time combination jobs
- Seasonal work
- Project-based employment
- Self-employment
- Cooperative businesses
- Remote work
- Flexible scheduling

Building Toward Independence: If you dream of self-employment but need stability:

1. Start side project while employed
2. Build financial cushion
3. Develop client base slowly
4. Test your capacity
5. Transition gradually

The Disability Option: In some cases, disability benefits might be appropriate:

- Document your work attempts
- Get professional opinions
- Understand the requirements
- Consider partial disability
- Plan for meaningful activity

This isn't giving up – it's recognizing your limitations and working within them.

Success Stories and Possibility Models

People with ADHD-BPD do succeed professionally, just differently:

The Entrepreneur Model: Use hyperfocus and intensity to build businesses, with support for administration

The Creative Model: Channel emotional intensity into art, writing, music, design

The Helper Model: Use empathy and understanding to excel in human services

The Specialist Model: Become expert in narrow areas that fascinate you

The Portfolio Model: Multiple part-time roles that together create fulltime income

The Supported Model: Traditional employment with significant accommodations and understanding

Your Career, Your Way

Professional success with ADHD-BPD doesn't look like neurotypical success. It's messier, less linear, more creative, often unconventional. You might never have the steady 30-year career with one company. You might never climb traditional ladders.

But you might create innovations others can't imagine. Build businesses around your obsessions. Help people from your deep well of experience. Create art from your intensity. Solve problems with your unique perspective.

The key is stopping the comparison to neurotypical careers and starting to build something that works for YOUR brain. That means honoring your limitations, leveraging your strengths, and creating structures that support your success.

Your career might be a winding path rather than a straight line. It might be a collage rather than a portrait. It might break every rule in the traditional playbook. But if it works for you, if it sustains you, if it allows you to contribute your gifts – then it's perfect.

Chapter 12: The Body Connection

Sleep, Exercise, and Feeding Your Dual Brain

Marcus used to think his physical health was separate from his mental health. Sure, he knew he should exercise and eat better, but those seemed like luxury concerns compared to just surviving each day with ADHD and BPD. Then he noticed a pattern: his worst emotional storms followed nights of poor sleep. His executive function completely collapsed when he forgot to eat. His rejection sensitivity skyrocketed when he stopped moving his body.

"I thought taking care of my body was optional," he told his therapist. "Like something I'd do once I got my mental health sorted. But it turns out my body IS my mental health. They're the same system."

This revelation changed his entire approach. Instead of seeing physical health as another thing to fail at, he started seeing it as medication he could control. Sleep became treatment. Exercise became therapy. Food became fuel for stability. Not perfect, not consistent, but fundamentally necessary.

Why Your Body Matters More Than Most People's

Everyone benefits from good physical health, but for ADHD-BPD brains, it's not optional enhancement – it's baseline survival. Here's why:

Your nervous system is more reactive. Both conditions involve heightened stress responses. Poor physical health amplifies this reactivity exponentially.

Your neurotransmitters are already struggling. ADHD involves dopamine issues. BPD affects serotonin. Both need proper nutrition and sleep to function at all.

Your emotional regulation depends on physical stability. Blood sugar crashes trigger emotional storms. Dehydration affects cognition. Exhaustion destroys distress tolerance.

Your executive function requires more resources. Your frontal lobe already works harder than neurotypical brains. Without proper fuel and rest, it simply stops working.

Your sensitivity extends to physical sensations. You feel physical discomfort more intensely, and it affects your emotional state more dramatically.

Sleep Hygiene for the Racing Mind and Storming Heart

Sleep with ADHD-BPD is a special kind of hell. ADHD keeps your mind spinning. BPD makes nighttime feel dangerous and lonely. Together, they create chronic insomnia that worsens everything.

The Wind-Down Sequence: Start 2-3 hours before intended sleep:

Hour 3: Last caffeine, finish intense tasks Hour 2: Dim lights, stop screens, begin routine Hour 1: Hygiene, meditation, reading Hour 0: In bed, sleep stories or breathing

The Racing Thoughts Protocol:

- Keep a notebook by bed for thought-dumping
- Use the "parking lot" technique (thoughts can wait until tomorrow)
- Listen to boring podcasts or audiobooks
- Count backwards from 300 by 3s
- Progressive muscle relaxation for physical tension

The Emotional Storm Night Plan: When emotions make sleep impossible:

1. Accept you might not sleep (pressure makes it worse)

2. Focus on rest, not sleep
3. Use crisis skills if needed
4. Try sleep meditation apps
5. Consider PRN medication if prescribed
6. Have a backup plan for tomorrow if you don't sleep

The ADHD Sleep Adaptations:
- Multiple alarms for bedtime routine
- Automated lights that dim
- Phone charging outside bedroom
- Weighted blanket for sensory input
- White noise or brown noise
- Cool room temperature (forces body to slow down)

Medication Timing:
- Stimulants early in the day only
- Mood stabilizers as prescribed (some cause drowsiness)
- Melatonin 2-3 hours before desired sleep
- Avoid alcohol (seems to help but worsens sleep quality)

Exercise as Medicine for Both Conditions

Exercise is basically free medication that treats both ADHD and BPD simultaneously. It:

- Increases dopamine (ADHD treatment)
- Regulates emotions (BPD treatment)
- Improves executive function
- Reduces stress hormones

- Provides sensory input
- Creates routine and structure

But traditional exercise advice doesn't work for ADHD-BPD brains.

The Movement Menu Approach: Instead of a rigid exercise plan, create options:

High Energy/Stable Mood:

- Running/intense cardio
- Kickboxing
- Dance classes
- Rock climbing

Low Energy/Stable Mood:

- Walking
- Gentle yoga
- Swimming
- Stretching

High Energy/Unstable Mood:

- Punching bag
- Sprint intervals
- Intense cleaning (yes, it counts)
- Aggressive gardening

Low Energy/Unstable Mood:

- Gentle movement in bed
- Seated stretches
- Brief walk outside

- Restorative yoga

The Ten-Minute Miracle: Can't commit to an hour? Don't. Commit to ten minutes:

- Ten minutes is infinitely better than zero
- Often leads to longer sessions
- Builds habit without overwhelming
- Matches ADHD attention span
- Achievable even when dysregulated

Exercise for Emotional Regulation: Specific movements for specific emotions:

- Anger: High-intensity intervals, boxing
- Anxiety: Steady-state cardio, walking
- Depression: Any movement, preferably outdoors
- Emptiness: Group classes, team activities
- Overwhelm: Yoga, tai chi, swimming

Nutrition for the Dual Diagnosis Brain

Food affects ADHD and BPD dramatically. Blood sugar swings trigger emotional storms. Nutrient deficiencies worsen symptoms. But executive dysfunction makes meal planning nearly impossible.

The Survival Nutrition Strategy: Perfect nutrition is impossible. Good-enough nutrition is achievable:

Always Available Foods:

- Protein shakes/bars
- Pre-cut vegetables
- Individual cheese portions

- Nuts and seeds
- Whole grain crackers
- Fruit that doesn't require preparation

The Emergency Meal System: Keep 5-10 emergency meals always available:

- Frozen dinners (healthier versions)
- Instant oatmeal with protein powder
- Canned soup with added vegetables
- Pre-made sandwiches
- Meal replacement shakes

Blood Sugar Stability Protocol:

- Eat protein with every meal/snack
- Small frequent meals over large ones
- Always carry emergency snacks
- Set eating alarms if you forget
- Never go more than 4 hours without food

The Safe Foods List: During emotional storms, you need foods that:

- Require zero preparation
- Provide comfort without crash
- You'll actually eat
- Won't trigger shame
- Give quick energy

Keep these ALWAYS available, no judgment.

Supplements That Might Help: (Always consult with healthcare providers)

- Omega-3s for brain function
- Magnesium for anxiety
- Vitamin D for mood
- B-complex for energy
- Probiotics for gut-brain health

Substance Use Risks and Harm Reduction

Let's be real: 78% of people with BPD have substance use issues. Add ADHD's dopamine-seeking, and substance use becomes extremely high risk. But shame and abstinence-only approaches often backfire.

Understanding Your Vulnerability:

- ADHD seeks stimulation through substances
- BPD uses substances for emotional regulation
- Both conditions involve impulsivity
- Rejection or failure can trigger use
- Substances temporarily mask symptoms

Harm Reduction Strategies: If you're using substances:

- Track patterns between use and symptoms
- Notice what you're medicating
- Use safer substances (marijuana over opioids)
- Set limits before you start
- Have accountability partners
- Never use alone if using dangerous substances

- Keep naloxone if using opioids

The Substitution Strategy: Replace substances with safer alternatives:

- Alcohol → Kava tea, CBD
- Stimulants → Coffee, intense exercise
- Marijuana → CBD, meditation
- Cigarettes → Nicotine replacement, fidgets
- Food → Gum, tea, movement

Getting Help Without Shame:

- Find providers who understand dual diagnosis
- Look for harm reduction programs
- Consider medication-assisted treatment
- Join support groups for neurodivergent people
- Be honest about what you're medicating

Creating Sustainable Routines

The all-or-nothing pattern is real: perfect adherence followed by complete collapse. Sustainable routines work with this pattern, not against it.

The Minimum Baseline: Define the absolute minimum for physical health:

- 6 hours in bed (even if not sleeping)
- One meal with protein
- 10 minutes of movement
- Medications taken
- Water consumed

The Flexible Routine Structure: Morning: Check-in with body, medications, fuel Midday: Movement break, meal, hydration Evening: Wind-down routine, preparation for tomorrow

Within this structure, infinite flexibility.

The Habit Stacking Method: Attach new habits to existing ones:

- Medication with morning coffee
- Stretches while coffee brews
- Protein shake after medication
- Walk after lunch
- Sleep routine after dinner

The Recovery Protocol: When routines collapse (they will):

1. No shame spiraling
2. Return to minimum baseline
3. Add one element at a time
4. Celebrate small returns
5. Adjust expectations

Body Doubling for Health Habits:

- Virtual workout buddies
- Meal prep parties
- Sleep routine accountability
- Walking partners
- Gym buddies who understand

The Integration of Physical and Mental Health

Stop thinking of physical health as separate from mental health. For ADHD-BPD, they're completely integrated:

Physical Symptoms as Warning Signs:

- Exhaustion → Emotional storm brewing
- Hunger → Executive function declining
- Tension → Anxiety building
- Restlessness → Need for movement/stimulation

Physical Health as Treatment:

- Sleep = mood stabilizer
- Exercise = antidepressant
- Nutrition = cognitive enhancement
- Hydration = emotional regulation
- Routine = anxiety reduction

The Feedback Loop: Better physical health → Better symptom management → Easier to maintain physical health → Continuing improvement

Worse physical health → Worse symptoms → Harder to maintain physical health → Continuing decline

Your Body Is Your Foundation

Here's what nobody tells you about physical health with ADHD-BPD: it's both harder for you AND more important for you than for neurotypical people. That's unfair. It's also reality.

You can't afford to neglect your body. But you also can't maintain perfect healthy habits. The solution? Good-enough consistency with complete self-compassion.

Some weeks you'll exercise daily and meal prep like a champion. Some weeks you'll survive on protein bars and consider showering a victory. Both are okay. What matters is returning to baseline without shame, building sustainable minimums, and recognizing that taking care of your body IS taking care of your mental health.

Your body isn't another thing to manage on top of ADHD-BPD. It's the foundation that makes managing ADHD-BPD possible. The more you support your physical health – imperfectly, inconsistently, but persistently – the more stable everything else becomes.

Section IV: Building Your Life
Long-term Recovery and Growth

Chapter 13: Family Healing and Support Systems

The Rodriguez family sat in their therapist's office, all looking in different directions. Maria, diagnosed with ADHD and BPD at 32, had finally convinced her parents and siblings to come to a session. Her mother kept dabbing at her eyes. Her father stared at the wall. Her younger brother scrolled through his phone. Her sister sat rigid, arms crossed.

"We don't understand what we did wrong," her mother finally said. "We gave you everything we had."

Maria took a shaky breath. "I know you did. This isn't about blame. It's about understanding that my brain works differently, and our family patterns – the ones that work fine for everyone else – they hurt me without anyone meaning them to."

Her father finally looked at her. "So what do we do now? How do we... fix this?"

"We don't fix it," the therapist interjected gently. "We heal it. Together. With everyone learning new ways to connect."

That session was the beginning of a two-year journey that transformed not just Maria's relationship with her family, but revealed that her father likely had undiagnosed ADHD, her mother showed signs of anxiety disorders, and the whole family system had been organized around managing unnamed neurodivergence for generations.

When Neurodivergence Runs in Families

Here's something that might blow your mind: ADHD and BPD don't just appear randomly. They cluster in families. If you have both conditions, there's a high probability that other family members have one or both conditions too, diagnosed or not.

This creates layers of complexity:

- Parents with undiagnosed ADHD trying to provide structure they can't maintain
- Siblings with their own emotional regulation challenges
- Grandparents from generations when these conditions weren't recognized
- Family systems organized around unnamed symptoms
- Intergenerational trauma patterns
- Genetic vulnerability meeting environmental triggers

The family that seems "normal" to outsiders might actually be a complex system of people all trying to manage neurodivergence without knowing that's what they're doing.

Educating Family Without Overwhelming Them

Your family probably has their own ideas about what's "wrong" with you. Maybe they think you're dramatic, lazy, selfish, or broken. Maybe they blame themselves. Maybe they deny there's anything different about you at all. Education needs to meet them where they are.

The Graduated Disclosure Method:

Start small. Don't dump everything at once.

Week 1: "I've been diagnosed with some conditions that affect how my brain works."

Week 2: "One is ADHD, which affects my focus and organization."

Week 3: "The other is BPD, which affects my emotions and relationships."

Week 4: "They're both neurological conditions, not character flaws."

Week 5: "Here's one article that explains it well..."

The Translation Approach:

Translate clinical language into family language:

- Instead of "emotional dysregulation," say "my feelings get very intense very fast"
- Instead of "executive dysfunction," say "my brain has trouble organizing and starting tasks"
- Instead of "rejection sensitive dysphoria," say "criticism feels physically painful to me"
- Instead of "identity disturbance," say "I have trouble knowing who I am sometimes"

The Concrete Examples Method:

Use specific family situations they'll recognize:

- "You know how I always interrupt at dinner? That's the ADHD impulsivity."
- "You know how I had meltdowns over small changes in plans? That's the BPD need for stability."
- "You know how I started twelve hobbies and finished none? That's both conditions affecting follow-through."

What to Share, What to Keep Private:

You don't owe your family every detail. Share:

- Basic information about both conditions
- How symptoms affect family interactions
- What support would help
- Your treatment approach
- Hope for improvement

Keep private (unless you choose otherwise):

- Specific trauma memories
- Self-harm details
- Sexual or romantic struggles
- Medication specifics
- Therapy content

Healing From Invalidating Environments

Many families, even loving ones, create invalidating environments for neurodivergent children. Not from malice, but from misunderstanding.

Common invalidating patterns:

- "You're too sensitive" (emotional invalidation)
- "You're not trying hard enough" (effort invalidation)
- "You just want attention" (need invalidation)
- "Why can't you be like your sister?" (identity invalidation)
- "Stop making excuses" (struggle invalidation)

These messages become internal voices that maintain both conditions. Healing requires recognizing these patterns without necessarily getting family to admit fault.

The Both/And Approach: "My parents loved me AND didn't understand my neurodivergence." "They did their best AND their best caused some harm." "They were good parents AND I needed different parenting." "I can love them AND protect myself from invalidation."

Setting Boundaries Around Invalidation:

Script: "I know you don't mean to hurt me, but when you say X, it makes my symptoms worse. Could you try saying Y instead?"

Example: "When you say 'just calm down,' my brain literally can't. Could you say 'I see you're struggling' instead?"

If they can't stop invalidating:

- Limit discussion of your conditions
- Reduce contact during vulnerable times
- Seek validation elsewhere
- Practice internal validation

Parenting With BPD-ADHD

If you're a parent with both conditions, you face unique challenges. Your symptoms can affect your children, but you're not doomed to harm them.

The Honest Age-Appropriate Approach:

Young children: "Mommy's brain gets big feelings sometimes. It's not your fault."

School age: "I have conditions that make some things harder for me. I'm working on them."

Teens: "I have ADHD and BPD. Here's what that means for our family..."

Managing Symptoms Around Children:

Create safety protocols:

- Partner or support person who can tag in during crisis
- Safe space for you to regulate away from kids
- Explanation that your emotions aren't their responsibility
- Consistent reassurance that they're loved even when you're struggling

The Good Enough Parent Model:

You don't have to be perfect. You have to be:

- Consistent enough (not perfectly consistent)
- Emotionally available enough (not always available)
- Stable enough (not never dysregulated)
- Present enough (not always present)

Your children need to see you:

- Make mistakes and repair them
- Have emotions and manage them
- Struggle and seek help
- Be human and still loving

Protecting Children From Your Symptoms:

- Never make children responsible for your emotions
- Don't use them as therapists or confidants
- Shield them from adult details of your conditions
- Get them their own support if needed
- Model getting help as strength

Being Parented by Someone With Both

If your parent has ADHD-BPD, you might have experienced:

- Inconsistent rules and expectations
- Emotional storms that seemed to come from nowhere
- Feeling responsible for their emotions
- Chaos alternating with intense control
- Love that felt conditional on their mood

- Confusion about what was normal

Healing involves:

- Understanding their behavior as symptoms, not personal
- Recognizing you weren't responsible for managing them
- Grieving the parent you needed but didn't have
- Setting adult boundaries with them
- Finding your own healing path

Adult Child Boundaries:

- You're not obligated to be their therapist
- You can love them and limit contact
- Their crisis doesn't require your response
- You can break family patterns
- Your healing matters too

Building Chosen Family

Not all family is biological. Chosen family – people who become your family through connection rather than blood – can be especially important for people with ADHD-BPD.

Why Chosen Family Matters:

- They meet you as you are now, not who you were
- No childhood baggage or old patterns
- Can understand through shared experience
- Often includes other neurodivergent people
- Based on mutual choice, not obligation

Building Chosen Family:

- Support groups become ongoing connections
- Online communities develop into real friendships
- Treatment relationships evolve into peer support
- Shared interests create lasting bonds
- Crisis buddies become life witnesses

Maintaining Chosen Family:
- Be honest about your conditions
- Respect their boundaries too
- Don't expect them to be everything
- Celebrate chosen family rituals
- Acknowledge the relationship's importance

Creating Your Support Ecosystem

No one person or group can meet all your support needs. You need an ecosystem:

Inner Circle (3-5 people):
- Emergency contacts
- Crisis support
- Daily check-ins possible
- Know your full story
- Can handle intensity

Middle Circle (5-10 people):
- Regular support
- Activity partners
- Accountability buddies

- Know your conditions
- Provide stability

Outer Circle (10+ people):
- Casual connections
- Shared interest groups
- Professional supports
- Know some struggles
- Provide normalcy

Professional Circle:
- Therapist
- Psychiatrist
- Primary care doctor
- Case manager if needed
- Other treatment providers

Peer Circle:
- Support groups
- Online communities
- Recovery buddies
- Mentors and mentees

Family Meetings That Work

Regular family meetings prevent crisis-driven communication:

Structure for Success:
- Monthly or biweekly

- Time-limited (60-90 minutes)
- Rotating facilitator
- Written agenda
- Everyone gets speaking time
- Focus on solutions, not blame

Agenda Template:
1. Check-ins (5 minutes each)
2. Appreciations (what's working)
3. Challenges (what's not)
4. Problem-solving (one issue deeply)
5. Planning (upcoming needs)
6. Connection activity (game, meal)

Rules for Neurodivergent Families:
- Fidgets and movement allowed
- Breaks every 20 minutes
- Visual aids welcome
- Emotions are valid
- No shame for symptoms
- Progress over perfection

Support Group Navigation

Support groups can be lifelines, but finding the right one matters:

Types Available:
- NAMI Family Support Groups

- Adult Children groups
- ADHD support groups
- DBT skills groups
- Peer-led BPD groups
- Online communities
- Diagnosis-specific groups

Finding Your Fit:
- Try multiple groups
- Notice group culture
- Check facilitator style
- Assess member stability
- Evaluate safety level
- Consider online vs. in-person

Getting the Most From Groups:
- Attend consistently
- Share at your comfort level
- Listen more than you speak initially
- Exchange contacts carefully
- Respect confidentiality absolutely
- Take what helps, leave the rest

When Family Can't or Won't Understand

Sometimes, despite your best efforts, family can't or won't understand. This is painful but not uncommon.

Reasons for Resistance:

- Their own undiagnosed conditions
- Generational trauma patterns
- Cultural stigma
- Fear of being blamed
- Denial as protection
- Lack of emotional capacity

Grieving the Family You Need: It's okay to grieve:

- The understanding you won't get
- The support you deserve
- The validation you crave
- The easy relationships others have
- The family you wish you had

Creating Boundaried Connection: You might maintain connection with limits:

- Holiday visits but not weekly calls
- Group gatherings but not one-on-one
- Surface contact about safe topics
- Information diet about your conditions
- Emotional support sought elsewhere

When No Contact Is Necessary: Sometimes the healthiest choice is distance:

- Ongoing abuse or cruelty
- Refusal to respect boundaries
- Triggering of severe symptoms

- Sabotage of your recovery
- Danger to your children

No contact doesn't mean:

- You've failed
- You're unforgiving
- You're dramatic
- You don't love them
- You're wrong

It means you're protecting your recovery.

Family Patterns Can Change

Here's what's possible: Family patterns that have existed for generations can change. Not overnight, not without effort, but genuinely change. It might start with you – the identified patient, the "problem," the one who got diagnosed. Your healing can catalyze system-wide transformation.

Or it might not. Your family might stay exactly the same while you change. That's okay too. Your recovery isn't dependent on their understanding. Your healing isn't contingent on their validation. Your life can be full and meaningful regardless of their participation.

The goal isn't a perfect family. It's a workable relationship with family (biological or chosen) that supports your recovery. That might be deep healing with your birth family. It might be cordial distance with relatives and deep connection with chosen family. It might be something in between.

What matters is that you build a support system that sees you, understands you (or tries to), and supports your growth. Family healing is possible – sometimes with the family you were born into, always with the family you choose to create.

Chapter 14: Trauma, Resilience, and Post-Traumatic Growth

When Kai first heard the term "post-traumatic growth," they laughed bitterly. "Growth? From this mess? I can barely survive each day, and you're telling me I'm supposed to grow from trauma that broke my brain?"

Kai's story was complex: early neglect that set the stage for both ADHD and BPD to flourish, multiple traumas throughout childhood and adolescence, and then adult traumas that seemed attracted to their vulnerability like magnets. At 28, they felt like a collection of wounds held together by psychiatric medications and sheer stubbornness.

But three years later, Kai stood in front of a room full of trauma survivors, facilitating a peer support group. "I'm not grateful for my trauma," they said clearly. "I wouldn't wish it on anyone. But I can't deny that surviving it, processing it, and integrating it has made me into someone I actually respect. The growth isn't instead of the pain – it's because I faced the pain instead of letting it destroy me."

The Trauma Triad: ADHD, BPD, and PTSD

If you have ADHD and BPD, the statistics suggest you've also experienced trauma. Studies show:

- 57% of people with BPD also have PTSD
- People with ADHD are more likely to experience trauma
- Both conditions increase vulnerability to traumatic experiences
- Trauma can worsen both conditions' symptoms

But it's more complex than just having three separate conditions. They interweave:

ADHD increases trauma risk through:
- Impulsivity leading to dangerous situations
- Attention issues missing warning signs
- Hyperactivity attracting negative attention
- Social struggles creating isolation
- Academic/work failures creating chronic stress

BPD and trauma interconnect through:
- Early trauma contributing to BPD development
- Emotional dysregulation making trauma processing harder
- Attachment trauma reinforcing abandonment fears
- Identity confusion after identity-attacking trauma
- Self-harm as trauma response

PTSD amplifies both conditions:
- Hypervigilance worsens ADHD attention issues
- Emotional numbing complicates BPD emptiness
- Flashbacks trigger both conditions' symptoms
- Avoidance prevents skill development
- Dissociation interferes with treatment

Understanding Your Trauma Layers

Trauma with ADHD-BPD often has multiple layers:

Pre-verbal trauma: Things that happened before you could speak or remember clearly, but shaped your nervous system

Developmental trauma: Ongoing childhood experiences that disrupted normal development

Acute trauma: Specific incidents (assault, accidents, losses) that created PTSD

Complex trauma: Multiple traumas over time, often in relationships meant to be safe

Systemic trauma: Oppression, discrimination, poverty, marginalization

Medical trauma: From treatments, hospitalizations, misdiagnoses

Neurodivergent trauma: From living in a world not built for your brain

Each layer needs different healing approaches. You might be simultaneously processing:

- A specific assault (EMDR for acute trauma)
- Childhood neglect (attachment therapy for developmental trauma)
- Lifetime of being misunderstood (validation for neurodivergent trauma)
- Societal oppression (justice-oriented therapy for systemic trauma)

Building Resilience With Dual Challenges

Resilience doesn't mean being unaffected by trauma. It means developing the capacity to navigate trauma's effects while building a meaningful life. With ADHD-BPD, resilience looks different:

Traditional resilience says: Bounce back quickly **ADHD-BPD resilience says**: Take the time you need, expect setbacks

Traditional resilience says: Stay stable under pressure **ADHD-BPD resilience says**: Fall apart safely, then rebuild

Traditional resilience says: Don't let it affect you **ADHD-BPD resilience says**: Feel it fully, then choose your response

Building Your Specific Resilience:

Biological resilience:

- Medication that addresses all conditions
- Sleep as non-negotiable medicine
- Movement for nervous system regulation
- Nutrition for neurotransmitter support
- Substances avoided or harm-reduced

Psychological resilience:

- Trauma-informed therapy
- DBT skills for emotional storms
- ADHD strategies for daily function
- Self-compassion practices
- Meaning-making activities

Social resilience:

- Support system that understands trauma
- Connections with other survivors
- Professional team that collaborates
- Chosen family who accepts you
- Community involvement as you're able

Spiritual resilience (however you define it):

- Connection to something larger
- Sense of purpose from survival
- Helping others as meaning-making

- Nature, art, music as transcendence
- Cultural practices that ground you

Post-Traumatic Growth Is Real

Post-traumatic growth isn't toxic positivity. It's not "everything happens for a reason" or "trauma makes you stronger." It's the observable fact that some people experience genuine growth after trauma processing. With ADHD-BPD, growth might look like:

Increased appreciation for life: When you've survived wanting to die, everyday moments can become precious

Deeper relationships: Trauma can strip away superficiality, leading to more authentic connections

Recognition of strength: Surviving with multiple conditions proves your resilience

New life priorities: Trauma clarifies what actually matters

Spiritual development: Questions trauma raises can lead to deeper meaning

Expanded empathy: Your pain can increase compassion for others' struggles

This growth doesn't happen instead of suffering – it happens through processing suffering with support.

Meaning-Making With Neurodivergence

Making meaning from trauma when your brain works differently requires adapted approaches:

The Non-Linear Narrative: Your trauma story might not be chronological or coherent. That's okay. ADHD affects memory sequencing. BPD affects identity continuity. Your narrative might be:

- Fragments that slowly connect

- Themes rather than timeline
- Emotions rather than events
- Body sensations rather than words
- Art rather than prose

The Multiple Meanings: With identity fluctuations, trauma might mean different things at different times:

- Sometimes it's the villain that destroyed you
- Sometimes it's the teacher that shaped you
- Sometimes it's just something that happened
- Sometimes it's the origin of your purpose
- All meanings can be simultaneously true

The Neurodivergent Lens: Your trauma might be complicated by being neurodivergent:

- Trauma from being punished for ADHD symptoms
- Trauma from being invalidated for BPD emotions
- Trauma from not fitting in anywhere
- Trauma from systems meant to help
- Making meaning requires acknowledging this specific pain

Cultural Trauma and Systemic Barriers

If you're marginalized in other ways, trauma becomes even more complex:

Intersectional trauma includes:

- Racial trauma + neurodivergent trauma
- Gender-based violence + mental health stigma

- Poverty trauma + lack of treatment access
- Cultural invalidation + family rejection
- Immigration trauma + language barriers
- All intersecting with ADHD-BPD

Healing requires acknowledging:

- Individual healing isn't enough if systems remain traumatic
- Your trauma might be ongoing, not past
- Cultural approaches might conflict with Western treatment
- Safety might be limited by systemic oppression
- Resilience includes resistance

Finding culturally responsive healing:

- Therapists who understand your identities
- Healing practices from your culture
- Community healing alongside individual
- Political action as therapeutic
- Reclaiming traditional practices

The Trauma-Informed Life

Living trauma-informed with ADHD-BPD means:

Recognizing triggers: Not just avoiding them but understanding them

- ADHD forgetfulness isn't carelessness
- BPD reactions might be trauma responses
- Both conditions affect trigger management

Creating safety: Internal and external

- Safe people who understand all conditions
- Safe spaces for processing
- Safe activities for regulation
- Safe boundaries with unsafe people
- Safe relationship with yourself

Practicing choice: Trauma removes choice; healing restores it

- Choose your healing pace
- Choose your disclosure level
- Choose your treatment approach
- Choose your meaning-making
- Choose your growth direction

Trauma Recovery Isn't Linear

With ADHD-BPD, trauma recovery is especially non-linear:

Monday: "I've healed so much, I'm amazing" Tuesday: "I'm broken beyond repair" Wednesday: "Maybe I'm okay" Thursday: Full trauma response to minor trigger Friday: Breakthrough in therapy Weekend: Complete exhaustion

This isn't failure. This is the pattern. Your executive dysfunction means you can't maintain consistent healing practices. Your emotional dysregulation means feelings about trauma will fluctuate wildly. Progress happens in spirals, not straight lines.

Building Your Trauma Recovery Plan

Assessment Phase:

- What traumas am I carrying?
- How do they interact with ADHD/BPD?

- What's helped before?
- What's made things worse?
- What am I ready to face?

Stabilization Phase:
- Get symptoms manageable
- Build support system
- Develop coping skills
- Create safety
- Establish routines

Processing Phase:
- Work with trauma-informed therapist
- Process at sustainable pace
- Use multiple modalities
- Allow integration time
- Expect temporary destabilization

Integration Phase:
- Make meaning from experiences
- Build new identity including growth
- Share story as you choose
- Help others if called
- Celebrate survival

Maintenance Phase:
- Ongoing support for all conditions

- Regular check-ins with self
- Adjusted expectations
- Continued growth
- Vigilance for new traumas

Your Trauma Doesn't Define Your Future

Yes, trauma shaped you. Yes, it complicated your ADHD and BPD. Yes, it might have broken you in ways that will never fully heal. And yes, you can still build a meaningful, connected, purposeful life.

Post-traumatic growth with ADHD-BPD isn't about becoming neurotypical or trauma-free. It's about integrating all parts of your experience into a whole that makes sense to you. It's about finding meaning not despite your suffering but through surviving it. It's about using your unique understanding to contribute something only you can contribute.

Your trauma doesn't define your future, but your healing might. The sensitivity that makes you vulnerable also makes you capable of profound growth. The intensity that overwhelms you also drives deep transformation. The complexity that exhausts you also creates rich wisdom.

You're not broken. You're surviving with remarkable resilience in a brain and world that make survival difficult. That's not just strength – that's the foundation for post-traumatic growth that can transform not just your life but the lives of others who need to see that healing is possible.

Chapter 15: Life Transitions and Major Decisions

Alex sat in their apartment surrounded by three whiteboards, seventeen sticky notes, and what appeared to be the world's most complex decision tree about whether to accept a job offer in another city. They'd been "deciding" for three weeks, cycling between absolute certainty (at 3 AM) and complete confusion (by noon), with their emotions and executive function taking turns sabotaging any attempt at clarity.

"The thing is," Alex explained to their therapist over video call, "my ADHD brain sees infinite possibilities and can't prioritize them. My BPD brain makes every option feel like life or death. Together, they've turned a simple job decision into an existential crisis that might actually trigger a real crisis if I don't figure this out soon."

The therapist nodded. "What if we stopped treating this like a neurotypical decision and started working with how your brain actually processes major choices?"

That reframe changed everything. Alex learned that life transitions with ADHD-BPD require completely different strategies than standard decision-making advice suggests.

Why Transitions Hit Different

Everyone struggles with life transitions, but ADHD-BPD creates specific vulnerabilities:

ADHD challenges with transitions:

- Executive dysfunction makes planning nearly impossible
- Time blindness means you can't accurately imagine future states

- Hyperfocus on certain aspects while missing others
- Impulsivity leads to sudden decisions or paralysis
- Working memory issues mean losing track of important factors
- Difficulty with sequential planning

BPD challenges with transitions:

- Identity confusion makes knowing what you want difficult
- Fear of abandonment activated by any change
- Emotional dysregulation during uncertainty
- Black-and-white thinking about options
- Splitting on current vs. future situations
- Emptiness and dissociation when faced with change

Combined, they create:

- Analysis paralysis alternating with impulsive choices
- Emotional flooding that shuts down logical thinking
- Identity crisis triggered by any major decision
- Abandonment panic about leaving or being left
- Executive function collapse from emotional overwhelm
- Decisions unmade and remade endlessly

Emerging Adulthood With BPD-ADHD

The transition from adolescence to adulthood is especially brutal with dual diagnosis. Traditional milestones become mountains:

The College Question: Standard path says: Go at 18, graduate at 22 Your path might be: Start at 18, drop out at 19, return at 23, change majors four times, graduate at 28, or find success without degree

The Career Launch: Standard path says: Entry-level to management in linear progression Your path might be: Multiple false starts, lateral moves, complete pivots, entrepreneurship, portfolio career, or non-traditional success

The Relationship Evolution: Standard path says: Date, commit, marry, children (if wanted) Your path might be: Intense connections, multiple breakups, chosen family, alternative relationship structures, or solo happiness

The Independence Journey: Standard path says: Move out, become financially independent, never return Your path might be: Multiple moves home, financial interdependence, creative living situations, or supported independence

None of these alternative paths mean failure. They mean adapting life to work with your neurodivergence.

Relationship Milestones and Commitments

Relationship transitions trigger both conditions maximally:

Moving In Together: The excitement (ADHD dopamine) meets abandonment fear (BPD), creating chaos:

- Pack at the last minute in dysregulated panic
- Idealize living together then catastrophize
- Forget important logistics while obsessing over emotional meaning
- Identity crisis about "who am I in this home?"

Strategy: Extended transition period. Keep separate spaces initially. Move gradually. Process emotions daily. Plan logistics with support.

Marriage/Commitment Ceremonies:

- ADHD: Overwhelm at planning, forgetting important details

- BPD: Terror of abandonment or engulfment, identity confusion
- Both: Family dynamics triggering symptoms

Strategy: Simple ceremony, long engagement, therapy throughout, clear boundaries with family, focus on relationship not event.

Having Children:

- Executive function challenges with baby care
- Emotional dysregulation with sleep deprivation
- Identity shift to "parent" triggering crisis
- Fear of repeating trauma patterns

Strategy: Extensive support system, realistic expectations, continued treatment, partner involvement, self-compassion.

Breakups/Divorce:

- Complete dysregulation from abandonment
- Executive dysfunction making logistics impossible
- Identity crisis from relationship loss
- Impulsive decisions during emotional flooding

Strategy: Therapist support essential, no major decisions for 6 months, structured separation process, maintained routines, crisis plan activated.

Educational and Vocational Transitions

School and work transitions require special consideration:

Returning to School:

- Part-time might be more sustainable than full-time
- Online or hybrid might work better than in-person

- Accommodations are essential, not optional
- Multiple attempts are normal, not failure

Career Changes:
- Driven by boredom (ADHD) or relationship issues (BPD)
- Require financial planning for instability
- Benefit from gradual transition
- Need identity work alongside practical planning

Retirement/Disability:
- Loss of structure catastrophic for ADHD
- Loss of identity devastating for BPD
- Requires extensive preparation
- Needs replacement structure and purpose

Managing Moves, Losses, and Changes

Physical moves and losses trigger cascading symptoms:

Moving Locations: Physical move means:
- Losing routine (ADHD crisis)
- Losing support system (BPD crisis)
- Executive function overwhelm
- Emotional dysregulation
- Identity confusion

Survival strategies:
- Start planning months in advance
- Visit new location multiple times

- Set up support system before moving
- Maintain some routines
- Give yourself adjustment time

Losing People (death, estrangement): Grief with ADHD-BPD is complicated:

- Can't process linearly
- Emotions overwhelming
- Executive function collapses
- Abandonment trauma activated
- Identity questions raised

Healing approaches:

- Extended grief timeline
- Multiple processing modalities
- Medication adjustments
- Increased support
- Meaning-making when ready

Decision-Making Frameworks for Complexity

Standard decision-making assumes neurotypical processing. You need adapted frameworks:

The Three-Brain Check: Before major decisions, check with:

1. Emotional brain: How does this feel?
2. Logical brain: What makes sense?
3. Body brain: What does my gut say?

Only proceed when at least 2/3 align.

The Values Compass: When identity is unclear, navigate by values:

- List top 5 values (freedom, connection, creativity, etc.)
- Rate each option against values
- Choose highest value alignment
- Accept imperfection

The Minimum Viable Decision: Instead of perfect choice:

- What's the smallest step forward?
- What's reversible?
- What can I try temporarily?
- What preserves most options?

The Support Council: Gather trusted advisors:

- Someone who knows your patterns
- Someone who's objective
- Someone who's been there
- Someone who'll support any choice

Present options, gather input, but YOU decide.

The Both/And Option: Black-and-white thinking says choose A or B. Creative thinking asks:

- Can I do both sequentially?
- Can I combine them?
- Can I try one with exit strategy?
- Can I create option C?

Planning Transitions With Flexibility

Rigid plans fail with ADHD-BPD. Flexible planning works:

The Wave Timeline: Instead of fixed deadlines:
- Wave 1: Preparation phase (flexible duration)
- Wave 2: Transition phase (expected chaos)
- Wave 3: Adjustment phase (longer than others need)
- Wave 4: Integration phase (new normal)

The Safety Net Planning: For every major transition, identify:
- Financial safety net
- Emotional support team
- Practical backup plans
- Crisis response protocol
- Exit strategy if needed

The Energy Budget: Transitions consume energy. Budget for:
- 50% regular capacity during transition
- Extra therapy sessions
- Increased medication needs
- More rest required
- Simplified other areas

When Decisions Feel Impossible

Sometimes ADHD-BPD makes decisions literally impossible:

Signs you need help:
- Cycling through same options for weeks
- Physical symptoms from stress
- Unable to think about anything else

- Relationships suffering from indecision
- Missing important deadlines

Getting unstuck:

- Set artificial deadline
- Flip a coin (notice your reaction)
- Ask someone else to decide
- Choose the reversible option
- Accept good enough
- Try therapy specifically for this

The Permission Slip: Give yourself permission to:

- Make imperfect decisions
- Change your mind
- Need more time
- Ask for help
- Avoid some transitions
- Do things differently

Creating Successful Transitions

Despite the challenges, successful transitions are possible:

Jason's Story: Five job changes led to freelance career that honors his cycling interests

Maria's Path: Three college attempts resulted in perfect-fit trade school and thriving business

Sam's Journey: Multiple relationships taught them about polyamory, where their intensity works

Alex's Decision: That job offer? They negotiated remote work, kept their support system, and made it work

Each found success by:

- Accepting their non-linear path
- Building support before transitions
- Planning for their neurodivergence
- Allowing longer adjustment periods
- Celebrating unconventional wins

Your Timeline Is Your Own

Life transitions with ADHD-BPD will never look like neurotypical transitions. You might take longer, try multiple times, need more support, choose different paths, or avoid some transitions entirely.

This isn't failure – it's adaptation. Your brain needs different conditions to navigate change successfully. When you provide those conditions – time, support, flexibility, self-compassion – you can navigate transitions that once seemed impossible.

Major decisions don't have to be made perfectly or permanently. They just have to be made in ways that honor your neurodivergence and support your growth. Sometimes the best decision is the one that preserves the most options. Sometimes it's the one that feels safest. Sometimes it's the one that scares you in a good way.

Your life doesn't have to follow anyone else's timeline or pattern. It just has to work for your unique brain and circumstances.

Chapter 16: Recovery Is Real - Long-Term Success with BPD-ADHD

Ten years ago, Taylor was homeless, cycling through psychiatric hospitals, and convinced they'd never see thirty. Their ADHD and BPD seemed like a death sentence written in neurotransmitters and childhood trauma. Every day was crisis. Every relationship was chaos. Every attempt at stability crumbled.

Today, Taylor runs a peer support program, maintains stable housing, has relationships that last, and hasn't been hospitalized in four years. "I still have both conditions," they tell the newly diagnosed people who attend their groups. "My brain still works differently. I still take medication, go to therapy, and use my skills daily. But recovery? Recovery is absolutely real."

Taylor's story isn't unique. Research shows that 50-70% of people with BPD achieve remission of symptoms. Add proper ADHD treatment, and outcomes improve further. The tragedy isn't that recovery is impossible – it's that so many people don't know it's possible.

What Recovery Actually Looks Like

Recovery from ADHD-BPD doesn't mean cure. It doesn't mean becoming neurotypical. It doesn't mean never struggling again. Real recovery looks like:

Symptom Remission, Not Elimination:

- Emotions still intense but not overwhelming
- Attention still variable but manageable
- Relationships still challenging but sustainable
- Identity still fluid but acceptable

- Impulsivity still present but controlled

Functional Improvement:
- Maintaining housing (even if messy)
- Sustaining work (even if non-traditional)
- Keeping relationships (even if complicated)
- Managing daily life (even if differently)
- Contributing to community (in your own way)

Quality of Life:
- More good days than bad
- Hope for the future
- Meaning and purpose
- Connections that matter
- Moments of genuine joy

Clinical Recovery Markers: Studies show people in recovery often:
- No longer meet full diagnostic criteria for BPD
- Have significantly reduced ADHD impairment
- Experience fewer hospitalizations
- Report improved life satisfaction
- Maintain gains over time

But here's the crucial part: recovery looks different for everyone.

Recovery Statistics That Should Give You Hope

The long-term studies on BPD are remarkably encouraging:
- By 10 years, 50% no longer meet diagnostic criteria

- By 16 years, that number rises to 70-80%
- 90% achieve symptomatic remission for at least 2 years
- Remission tends to be stable once achieved

For ADHD:
- 70% of adults respond well to medication
- Combined medication and therapy shows best outcomes
- Executive function can improve throughout adulthood
- Coping strategies become more effective over time

When both are treated together:
- Integrated treatment improves outcomes for both
- Medication compliance is better
- Skill implementation improves
- Crisis episodes decrease
- Functioning steadily improves

These aren't miracle cures. They're people learning to work with their brains rather than against them.

The Recovery Journey Stages

Recovery happens in stages, often non-linearly:

Stage 1: Crisis Stabilization (Months to Years)
- Getting out of immediate danger
- Basic medication management
- Learning fundamental coping skills
- Establishing any support system
- Surviving each day

Stage 2: Skill Building (1-3 Years)

- DBT or other therapy engagement
- ADHD management strategies
- Building routine and structure
- Developing emotional regulation
- Creating stability

Stage 3: Identity Development (2-5 Years)

- Understanding yourself beyond diagnosis
- Exploring values and goals
- Building authentic relationships
- Finding meaning and purpose
- Accepting neurodivergence

Stage 4: Integration (Ongoing)

- Symptoms become manageable background
- Life expands beyond illness
- Helping others in earlier stages
- Continued growth and development
- Living with rather than despite conditions

Stage 5: Thriving (Possible for Many)

- Genuinely good quality of life
- Stable relationships and work
- Sense of self-efficacy
- Contributing to community

- Wisdom from experience

You might cycle through stages, skip some, or experience them simultaneously.

Maintaining Gains and Preventing Relapse

Recovery isn't a achievement you unlock permanently. It requires ongoing maintenance:

The Maintenance Non-Negotiables:

- Medication consistency (if using)
- Regular therapy or support
- Sleep protection
- Stress management
- Relationship boundaries
- Physical health basics

Relapse Prevention Planning: Know your warning signs:

- Sleep disruption increasing
- Medication "forgetting" starting
- Isolation creeping in
- Old patterns returning
- Therapy resistance growing

Have response protocols:

- Early warning: Increase self-care
- Yellow zone: Contact support system
- Orange zone: Emergency therapy session
- Red zone: Crisis plan activation

The Setback Reframe: Setbacks aren't failure. They're information:

- What triggered this?
- What helped before?
- What needs adjustment?
- What support is missing?
- What can I learn?

Every setback survived is proof of resilience.

Building a Life Worth Living

This phrase from DBT becomes especially meaningful in recovery. A life worth living with ADHD-BPD might include:

Meaningful Work (Paid or Unpaid):

- Using your lived experience to help others
- Creative expression of your intensity
- Project-based work matching attention cycles
- Part-time combination that works
- Volunteer work that matters

Sustaining Relationships:

- A few deep connections over many shallow
- Friends who understand mental health
- Family relationships (birth or chosen)
- Romantic partnership if desired
- Community connections

Personal Growth:

- Continued learning about yourself

- Skill development beyond symptom management
- Hobbies that bring joy
- Spiritual or philosophical exploration
- Creative pursuits

Contribution:
- Peer support work
- Advocacy for neurodivergent rights
- Art that expresses your experience
- Mentoring others
- Breaking stigma by living openly

Simple Pleasures:
- Morning coffee in peace
- A pet's unconditional love
- Favorite music
- Nature walks
- Good books
- Laughter with friends

Becoming an Advocate and Helper

Many people in recovery feel called to help others. Your lived experience is valuable:

Formal Peer Support:
- Certified peer specialist training
- Leading support groups
- Hospital peer support

- Warm line volunteering
- Crisis text counseling

Informal Support:
- Sharing your story openly
- Mentoring someone newer to recovery
- Online community participation
- Blog or social media advocacy
- Being visible in recovery

Professional Paths: Many with lived experience become:
- Therapists
- Social workers
- Psychiatric nurses
- Researchers
- Policy advocates

The Helper's Boundaries:
- You can't save everyone
- Your recovery comes first
- It's okay to take breaks
- Vicarious trauma is real
- Professional support for helpers exists

Success Stories From Real People

Maya, 42: "I haven't self-harmed in 6 years. I'm married, have two kids, and work part-time as a peer counselor. My house is chaotic, I still take five medications, and I have bad days. But I also have a life I never imagined possible."

James, 35: "Three degrees started and abandoned, twelve jobs, two divorces. Then proper diagnosis and treatment. Now I run my own business that works with my brain, not against it. Success looks different than I imagined, but it's still success."

Li, 28: "I thought I'd be dead by 25. Now I'm in graduate school, have friends who actually know me, and can handle emotions without destroying everything. Recovery isn't perfect, but it's real."

Carmen, 55: "Diagnosed at 48. Spent most of my life thinking I was fundamentally broken. Now I facilitate DBT groups and have the most stable relationship of my life. It's never too late."

Phoenix, 23: "Two years since my last hospitalization. I still live with my parents, can only work part-time, and need lots of support. But I'm alive, I'm growing, and I have hope. That's recovery for me."

Your Recovery Roadmap

Creating your personal recovery roadmap:

Where You Are Now:

- Current symptom severity
- Functional impairments
- Support available
- Treatment engaged
- Stability level

Where You Want to Be (Realistic Version):

- Symptom management goals
- Functional improvements desired
- Relationship hopes

- Work/activity goals
- Quality of life dreams

The Path Between:

- Treatment needed
- Skills to develop
- Support to build
- Changes to make
- Time to allow

Milestones to Celebrate:

- First week without crisis
- First month of medication compliance
- First successful boundary
- First healthy relationship
- First year of stability
- Every single victory

Recovery Is Not Only Possible But Probable

Here's what the research definitively shows: most people with BPD significantly improve over time. Add proper ADHD treatment, and functioning improves further. This isn't toxic positivity or false hope. This is data from long-term studies following real people with dual diagnoses.

Recovery doesn't mean easy. Your brain will always work differently. You'll always need more support than neurotypical people. You'll always have vulnerabilities. But you can absolutely build a life that feels worth living, relationships that sustain you, and days that contain more joy than suffering.

The path isn't straight. You might need multiple types of treatment. You might try dozens of medications. You might relapse, restart, relapse again. But each attempt teaches you something. Each recovery lasts a little longer. Each setback gets a little easier to overcome.

Ten years from now, you could be the one telling your story to someone who can't imagine surviving. You could be living proof that ADHD and BPD don't have to be a life sentence of suffering. You could be thriving in ways you can't currently imagine.

Recovery is real. It's happening for people with exactly your challenges. And with the right support, treatment, and time, it can happen for you too.

Appendices

Appendix A: Quick Reference Guides

Emergency Resources and Crisis Lines

When you're in crisis with ADHD and BPD, having resources immediately available can save your life. Here's what you need, organized for quick access even when your executive function is shot and emotions are overwhelming.

National Crisis Lines (USA):

- **988** - Suicide & Crisis Lifeline (call or text)
- **Text HOME to 741741** - Crisis Text Line
- **1-800-950-NAMI (6264)** - NAMI Helpline (Mon-Fri, 10am-10pm ET)
- **1-866-488-7386** - Trevor Project (LGBTQ+)
- **1-800-273-8255** - Veterans Crisis Line

International Crisis Resources:

- **UK**: 116 123 (Samaritans)
- **Canada**: 1-833-456-4566
- **Australia**: 13 11 14 (Lifeline)
- **Global**: findahelpline.com for country-specific resources

Warm Lines (Non-crisis peer support):

- **NAMI Warm Line Directory**: warmline.org
- Available for when you need support but aren't in immediate danger
- Staffed by peers who understand mental health challenges

Text-Based Support (for when talking is too hard):

- Crisis Text Line: Text HOME to 741741
- NAMI Text Line: Text NAMI to 741741
- IMAlive.org - online chat crisis support

Apps for Crisis Management:

- **Sanvello**: CBT-based coping tools
- **DBT Coach**: Skills for emotional crisis
- **notOK**: Alert your support network
- **MindShift**: Anxiety and panic management
- **Youper**: AI emotional support

When to Use Emergency Services: Call 911 or go to ER if:

- You have a specific suicide plan and means
- You've already harmed yourself significantly
- You're experiencing psychosis or severe dissociation
- You can't keep yourself safe
- Your support system agrees you need immediate help

Medication Reference Chart

Understanding your medications helps with compliance and advocacy. Here's a quick reference for common ADHD-BPD medications:

ADHD Medications:

Stimulants - Methylphenidate Based:

- **Ritalin/Methylin**: 2-4 hour duration, 2-3x daily
- **Concerta**: 12 hour duration, once daily

- **Daytrana Patch**: 9 hour duration, daily patch
- Common side effects: Appetite loss, sleep issues, increased heart rate

Stimulants - Amphetamine Based:

- **Adderall IR**: 4-6 hour duration, 2-3x daily
- **Adderall XR**: 10-12 hour duration, once daily
- **Vyvanse**: 10-14 hour duration, once daily
- Common side effects: Similar to methylphenidate, may cause more anxiety

Non-Stimulants:

- **Strattera (atomoxetine)**: Takes 4-6 weeks to work fully
- **Wellbutrin (bupropion)**: Also helps depression
- **Guanfacine/Clonidine**: Helps with hyperactivity and sleep
- Generally fewer side effects but less dramatic improvement

BPD Medications:

Mood Stabilizers:

- **Lamotrigine**: Slow titration required, helps emotional dysregulation
- **Valproic Acid**: Helps aggression and mood swings
- **Topiramate**: May help impulsivity, can affect cognition
- **Lithium**: Rarely used for BPD alone, requires blood monitoring

Antipsychotics (use cautiously):

- **Quetiapine**: Low doses for sleep/anxiety
- **Aripiprazole**: May help with aggression

- **Olanzapine**: For severe dysregulation
- Watch for metabolic side effects

Antidepressants (limited evidence for BPD):

- **SSRIs**: May help comorbid depression/anxiety
- **SNRIs**: Sometimes helpful for emotional pain
- Use cautiously - can increase impulsivity in some

Combination Considerations:

- Stimulant + mood stabilizer often helpful
- Monitor for interactions
- Start one medication at a time
- Document responses carefully
- Adjust based on symptom patterns

DBT Skills Cheat Sheet

When emotional dysregulation meets executive dysfunction, you need skills simplified to their essence:

TIPP (Crisis Survival):

- **T**emperature: Face in ice water 15-30 seconds
- **I**ntense Exercise: Sprint, jumping jacks for 1 minute
- **P**aced Breathing: In for 4, hold 4, out 6
- **P**aired Muscle Relaxation: Tense everything 5 seconds, release

STOP (Prevent Impulsivity):

- **S**top what you're doing
- **T**ake a step back

- **O**bserve the situation
- **P**roceed mindfully

PLEASE (Reduce Vulnerability):
- Treat **P**hysical illness
- Balance **L**ife/eating
- Avoid mood-**E**altering substances
- Balance **S**leep
- Get **E**xercise

DEAR MAN (Get What You Need):
- **D**escribe situation
- **E**xpress feelings/needs
- **A**ssert what you want
- **R**einforce benefits
- Stay **M**indful
- **A**ppear confident
- **N**egotiate

GIVE (Maintain Relationships):
- Be **G**entle
- Act **I**nterested
- **V**alidate
- Use **E**asy manner

FAST (Keep Self-Respect):
- Be **F**air

- No unnecessary **A**pologies
- **S**tick to values
- Be **T**ruthful

Wise Mind Quick Access:
- Emotion Mind: What am I feeling?
- Reasonable Mind: What are the facts?
- Wise Mind: What's the balanced response?

ADHD Accommodation Ideas

Workplace, school, and life accommodations that actually help:

Time Management:
- Extended deadlines with check-in points
- Buffer time between meetings/classes
- Flexible start times for peak focus
- Permission to be 5-10 minutes late
- Visual schedules and timers

Environment:
- Quiet workspace/testing environment
- Noise-canceling headphones permitted
- Reduced visual distractions
- Standing desk option
- Movement breaks every 30-60 minutes

Task Management:
- Written instructions for verbal directions

- Task broken into smaller components
- Priority assistance from supervisor
- Regular check-ins for accountability
- Project management software access

Communication:
- Email summaries of meetings
- Permission to record lectures/meetings
- Advance notice of changes
- Clear, direct feedback
- Regular one-on-ones

Memory Support:
- Note-taking assistance or technology
- Reminder systems approved
- Checklists and templates provided
- Important info in writing
- Access to meeting notes/recordings

School-Specific:
- Extended test time (1.5x or 2x)
- Separate testing location
- Breaks during exams
- Reduced course load
- Note-taker or recording permitted
- Assignment flexibility

Work-Specific:
- Work from home options
- Flexible scheduling
- Job coaching
- Modified training period
- Reduced interruptions
- Task reassignment for strengths

Daily Routine Templates

Routines for ADHD-BPD need to be flexible yet structured:

Morning Routine (Adjustable):

High Function Day (90 minutes):
- Wake with sunrise alarm
- Medication immediately
- 10 min movement/stretch
- Shower with music
- Breakfast with protein
- Review day's priorities
- Pack/prep for day
- Mindfulness moment before leaving

Medium Function Day (45 minutes):
- Wake with multiple alarms
- Medication with water by bed
- Quick rinse shower

- Grab-and-go breakfast
- Check calendar
- Basic hygiene
- Go

Low Function Day (20 minutes):

- Wake whenever
- Medication (set out night before)
- Face wash
- Protein bar
- Comfortable clothes
- Survival mode activated

Work/Productivity Routine:

Energy-Based Schedule:

- **High Energy**: Complex tasks, meetings
- **Medium Energy**: Routine tasks, emails
- **Low Energy**: Filing, organizing, planning
- **Crashed Energy**: Rest, self-care

Pomodoro Adapted:

- 15 min work → 5 min move
- 15 min work → 5 min breathe
- 15 min work → 10 min reward
- Repeat or rest

Evening Wind-Down:

2 Hours Before Bed:

- Last stimulating activity
- Prep tomorrow (clothes, meds, bag)
- Warm shower/bath
- Dim lights begin

1 Hour Before:

- No screens
- Calming activity (reading, music)
- Light snack if needed
- Journal thoughts out

30 Minutes Before:

- In bedroom
- Progressive relaxation
- Sleep story or meditation
- Gratitude practice

Weekend Routine Structure:

Saturday:

- Sleep in (but not past 10)
- Slow morning routine
- One "must do" task
- Social or fun activity
- Early dinner
- Relaxing evening

Sunday:
- Similar wake time to weekdays
- Meal prep (or order groceries)
- Week planning session
- Self-care activity
- Early bedtime prep

Appendix B: Resources for Families and Clinicians

Family Education Materials

Understanding Dual Diagnosis - Family Guide:

What's Happening in Their Brain:

- ADHD: Dopamine deficiency affecting focus and impulse control
- BPD: Emotional regulation disruption and attachment sensitivity
- Combined: Each condition amplifies the other
- This is neurobiology, not choice or character

What Families Often Misunderstand:

- "Attention-seeking" is actually attachment-seeking
- "Laziness" is actually executive dysfunction
- "Drama" is actually emotional dysregulation
- "Manipulation" is actually desperation
- "Not trying" is actually trying extremely hard

How to Help:

- Learn about both conditions
- Validate emotions while maintaining boundaries
- Provide structure without rigidity
- Offer support without enabling

- Take care of your own mental health

Communication Strategies:

- Use "I" statements about impact
- Avoid criticism of character
- Focus on specific behaviors
- Acknowledge their experience
- Set clear, consistent boundaries

Clinical Assessment Tools

Diagnostic Instruments:

For ADHD:

- Adult ADHD Self-Report Scale (ASRS-v1.1)
- Conners Adult ADHD Rating Scales (CAARS)
- DIVA 2.0 (Diagnostic Interview for ADHD in Adults)
- Brown ADD Scales
- Wender Utah Rating Scale (childhood symptoms)

For BPD:

- McLean Screening Instrument (MSI-BPD)
- Personality Diagnostic Questionnaire (PDQ-4)
- Structured Clinical Interview for DSM-5 (SCID-5-PD)
- Zanarini Rating Scale for BPD (ZAN-BPD)
- Borderline Evaluation of Severity over Time (BEST)

For Both/Differential Diagnosis:

- Minnesota Multiphasic Personality Inventory (MMPI-2)

- Millon Clinical Multiaxial Inventory (MCMI-IV)
- Personality Assessment Inventory (PAI)
- Clinical interview assessing developmental history
- Collateral information from family/partners

Treatment Planning Guides

Integrated Treatment Planning Steps:

1. **Comprehensive Assessment**:
    - Both conditions evaluated
    - Trauma history explored
    - Substance use assessed
    - Support system mapped
    - Strengths identified

2. **Prioritization**:
    - Safety first (self-harm, suicidality)
    - Substance use if present
    - Medication stabilization
    - Skills building
    - Trauma processing when stable

3. **Modality Selection**:
    - DBT for emotional dysregulation
    - CBT for ADHD management
    - Medication for both
    - Group and individual therapy

- Peer support integration

4. **Goal Setting**:
    - Short-term crisis management
    - Medium-term skill building
    - Long-term recovery vision
    - Functional improvements
    - Quality of life measures

Insurance and Advocacy Resources

Getting Coverage:

Documentation Needs:

- Both diagnoses clearly stated
- Functional impairments detailed
- Medical necessity explained
- Treatment history documented
- Provider recommendations specific

Appeal Process:

- First-level appeal within 30 days
- Include additional documentation
- Provider letter of medical necessity
- Peer-to-peer review request
- External review if needed

Resources:

- NAMI Insurance Resources

- Your state's insurance commissioner
- Patient advocacy organizations
- Mental Health America resources
- The Kennedy Forum for parity issues

Professional Development Recommendations

For Clinicians Treating ADHD-BPD:

Essential Trainings:

- DBT Intensive Training (Behavioral Tech)
- ADHD Assessment and Treatment (CHADD professional training)
- Trauma-Informed Care certification
- Dual Diagnosis treatment approaches
- Cultural competency in neurodiversity

Recommended Reading:

- Linehan's DBT manuals
- Barkley's ADHD handbooks
- Gunderson's BPD clinical guides
- Van der Kolk's trauma work
- Integration of treatment approaches

Ongoing Education:

- ISSPD (International Society for Study of Personality Disorders)
- APSARD (American Professional Society of ADHD and Related Disorders)

- ISST-D (International Society for Study of Trauma and Dissociation)
- Regular consultation groups
- Peer supervision for complex cases

Appendix C: Worksheets and Tools

Symptom Trackers

Daily Dual Diagnosis Tracker:

Date: _____

Morning Check-in:

- Mood (1-10): ___
- Energy (1-10): ___
- Focus (1-10): ___
- Anxiety (1-10): ___
- Medication taken: Y/N

Midday Check:

- Emotional storms: None/Minor/Major
- Executive function: Good/Fair/Poor
- Impulsive actions: None/Resisted/Acted
- Social interactions: Positive/Neutral/Difficult

Evening Review:

- Biggest challenge: _____
- Skills used: _____
- Success today: _____
- Tomorrow's priority: _____

Sleep:

- Bedtime: ___
- Estimated sleep: ___
- Quality: Good/Fair/Poor

Mood and Medication Logs

Weekly Medication & Mood Log:

Medication Tracking:
- Med 1: _____ Dose: _____ Time: _____
- Med 2: _____ Dose: _____ Time: _____
- Med 3: _____ Dose: _____ Time: _____
- PRN used: _____ Reason: _____

Mood Patterns:
- Monday: Morning___ Afternoon___ Evening___
- Tuesday: Morning___ Afternoon___ Evening___
- (Continue for week)

Notable Patterns:
- Best time of day: _____
- Worst time of day: _____
- Triggers noticed: _____
- What helped: _____

Relationship Mapping Exercise

Relationship Support Map:

Draw yourself in the center, then map:

Inner Circle (Emergency supports):

- Who: _____
- How they help: _____
- Contact info readily available: Y/N

Middle Circle (Regular support):

- Who: _____
- Type of support: _____
- Frequency of contact: _____

Outer Circle (Casual support):

- Who: _____
- Connection point: _____
- Potential for closer connection: Y/N

Professional Circle:

- Therapist: _____
- Psychiatrist: _____
- Other: _____

Reflection Questions:

- Where are the gaps?
- Who needs boundaries?
- Who could move circles?
- What support is missing?

Values Clarification Worksheet

Values for Variable Identity:

Core Values That Persist (circle all that apply):

- Connection
- Freedom
- Creativity
- Safety
- Growth
- Authenticity
- Contribution
- Adventure
- Stability
- Justice

How They Show Up: When stable: _____ When struggling: _____ In relationships: _____ In work: _____ In crisis: _____

Values Compass Creation: Top 3 values for decision-making:

1. _____
2. _____
3. _____

How current life aligns (1-10): Value 1: ___ Value 2: ___ Value 3: ___

One change to increase alignment: _____

Crisis Planning Template

My Crisis Response Plan:

Warning Signs I'm Approaching Crisis:

- Early: _____

- Middle: _____
- Late: _____

My Crisis Kit Location: _____

Contains:
- Ice pack
- Crisis contact list
- PRN medication
- Comfort items
- Skill cards
- Other: _____

My Crisis Response Steps:
1. STOP and breathe
2. Use TIPP skills
3. Contact: _____ (primary support)
4. If no response, contact: _____ (backup)
5. Use coping skill: _____
6. If still in crisis: _____

Professional Crisis Resources:
- Therapist crisis line: _____
- Local crisis center: _____
- Hospital preference: _____
- 988 for immediate support

Post-Crisis Recovery:

- Rest required: _____
- Check-in with: _____
- Therapy within: _____ days
- Gentle activities: _____
-

Using These Resources

These appendices aren't meant to be memorized or perfect. They're tools for when you need them. Some days, you'll use multiple resources. Some days, you won't need any. That's the nature of ADHD-BPD.

The key is having them available when your executive function can't create structure and your emotional dysregulation makes thinking impossible. Print what you need. Put copies everywhere. Share with support people. Modify to fit your life.

, and know that needing tools isn't weakness – it's wisdom.

Reference

American Psychiatric Association. (2013). *Diagnostic and statistical manual of mental disorders* (5th ed.). American Psychiatric Publishing.

Attention Deficit Disorder Association. (2023). *Workplace accommodations for ADHD*.

Behavioral Tech. (2023). *DBT resources and training*.

Biskin, R. S. (2015). The lifetime course of borderline personality disorder. *The Canadian Journal of Psychiatry*, *60*(7), 303-308.

Black, D. W., Blum, N., Pfohl, B., & Hale, N. (2004). Suicidal behavior in borderline personality disorder: Prevalence, risk factors, prediction, and prevention. *Journal of Personality Disorders*, *18*(3), 226-239.

Bohus, M., & Kröger, C. (2011). Psychopathology and psychotherapy of borderline personality disorder: State of the art. *Der Nervenarzt*, *82*(1), 16-24.

Borderline Personality Disorder Resource Center. (2023). *Family guidelines and education*.

CHADD (Children and Adults with Attention-Deficit/Hyperactivity Disorder). (2023). *Professional training and resources*.

Cloitre, M., Courtois, C. A., Ford, J. D., Green, B. L., Alexander, P., Briere, J., ... & Van der Hart, O. (2012). *The ISTSS expert consensus treatment guidelines for complex PTSD in adults*. International Society for Traumatic Stress Studies.

DBT Self Help. (2023). *DBT skills and resources*.

Distel, M. A., Trull, T. J., Derom, C. A., Thiery, E. W., Grimmer, M. A., Martin, N. G., ... & Boomsma, D. I. (2008). Heritability of borderline personality disorder features is similar across three countries. *Psychological Medicine*, *38*(9), 1219-1229.

Fonagy, P., Luyten, P., Allison, E., & Campbell, C. (2017). What we have changed our minds about: Part 1. Borderline personality disorder as a limitation of resilience. *Borderline Personality Disorder and Emotion Dysregulation*, *4*(1), 11.

Fossati, A., Madeddu, F., & Maffei, C. (1999). Borderline personality disorder and childhood sexual abuse: A meta-analytic study. *Journal of Personality Disorders*, *13*(3), 268-280.

Grant, B. F., Chou, S. P., Goldstein, R. B., Huang, B., Stinson, F. S., Saha, T. D., ... & Ruan, W. J. (2008). Prevalence, correlates, disability, and comorbidity of DSM-IV borderline personality disorder: Results from the Wave 2 National Epidemiologic Survey on Alcohol and Related Conditions. *The Journal of Clinical Psychiatry*, *69*(4), 533-545.

Gunderson, J. G., Stout, R. L., McGlashan, T. H., Shea, M. T., Morey, L. C., Grilo, C. M., ... & Skodol, A. E. (2011). Ten-year course of borderline personality disorder: Psychopathology and function from the Collaborative Longitudinal Personality Disorders study. *Archives of General Psychiatry*, *68*(8), 827-837.

Herman, J. L. (1992). Complex PTSD: A syndrome in survivors of prolonged and repeated trauma. *Journal of Traumatic Stress*, *5*(3), 377-391.

Hooley, J. M., & Hoffman, P. D. (1999). Expressed emotion and clinical outcome in borderline personality disorder. *American Journal of Psychiatry*, *156*(10), 1557-1562.

The International Society for the Study of Personality Disorders. (2023). *Professional resources and training*.

Job Accommodation Network. (2023). *Accommodation ideas for ADHD*

Joyce, P. R., McKenzie, J. M., Carter, J. D., Rae, A. M., Luty, S. E., Frampton, C. M., & Mulder, R. T. (2007). Temperament, character and personality disorders as predictors of response to interpersonal psychotherapy and cognitive-behavioural therapy for depression. *The British Journal of Psychiatry*, *190*(6), 503-508.

Kessler, R. C., McLaughlin, K. A., Green, J. G., Gruber, M. J., Sampson, N. A., Zaslavsky, A. M., ... & Williams, D. R. (2010). Childhood adversities and adult psychopathology in the WHO World Mental Health Surveys. *The British Journal of Psychiatry*, *197*(5), 378-385.

Lenzenweger, M. F., Lane, M. C., Loranger, A. W., & Kessler, R. C. (2007). DSM-IV personality disorders in the National Comorbidity Survey Replication. *Biological Psychiatry*, *62*(6), 553-564.

Linehan, M. M. (2015). *DBT skills training handouts and worksheets* (2nd ed.). Guilford Press.

Links, P. S., & Heslegrave, R. J. (2000). Prospective studies of outcome: Understanding mechanisms of change in patients with borderline personality disorder. *Psychiatric Clinics of North America*, *23*(1), 137-150.

McGlashan, T. H., Grilo, C. M., Sanislow, C. A., Ralevski, E., Morey, L. C., Gunderson, J. G., ... & Pagano, M. (2005). Two-year prevalence and stability of individual DSM-IV criteria for schizotypal, borderline, avoidant, and obsessive-compulsive personality disorders: Toward a hybrid model of axis II disorders. *American Journal of Psychiatry*, *162*(5), 883-889.

McLean Hospital. (2023). *BPD treatment planning guides*.

McLean, L. M., & Gallop, R. (2003). Implications of childhood sexual abuse for adult borderline personality disorder and complex posttraumatic stress disorder. *American Journal of Psychiatry*, *160*(2), 369-371.

National Alliance on Mental Illness. (2023). *Crisis resources and family education*.

National Suicide Prevention Lifeline. (2023). *988 Suicide and Crisis Lifeline resources*.

Paris, J. (2008). Clinical trials of treatment for personality disorders. *Psychiatric Clinics of North America*, *31*(3), 517-526.

Paris, J., & Zweig-Frank, H. (2001). A 27-year follow-up of patients with borderline personality disorder. *Comprehensive Psychiatry*, *42*(6), 482-487.

Psych Central. (2023). *ADHD daily routine templates and resources*.

Reich, D. B., & Zanarini, M. C. (2001). Developmental aspects of borderline personality disorder. *Harvard Review of Psychiatry*, *9*(6), 294-301.

Ruocco, A. C. (2005). The neuropsychology of borderline personality disorder: A meta-analysis and review. *Psychiatry Research*, *137*(1-2), 191-202.

Safren, S. A., Perlman, C. A., Sprich, S., & Otto, M. W. (2005). *Mastering your adult ADHD: A cognitive-behavioral treatment program*. Oxford University Press.

Skodol, A. E., Gunderson, J. G., Pfohl, B., Widiger, T. A., Livesley, W. J., & Siever, L. J. (2002). The borderline diagnosis I: Psychopathology, comorbidity, and personality structure. *Biological Psychiatry*, *51*(12), 936-950.

Substance Abuse and Mental Health Services Administration. (2023). *National helpline and treatment resources*.

Tedeschi, R. G., & Calhoun, L. G. (2004). Posttraumatic growth: Conceptual foundations and empirical evidence. *Psychological Inquiry*, *15*(1), 1-18.

Van der Kolk, B. A. (2014). *The body keeps the score: Brain, mind, and body in the healing of trauma.* Penguin Books.

Zanarini, M. C., Vujanovic, A. A., Parachini, E. A., Boulanger, J. L., Frankenburg, F. R., & Hennen, J. (2003). A screening measure for BPD: The McLean Screening Instrument for Borderline Personality Disorder (MSI-BPD). *Journal of Personality Disorders*, *17*(6), 568-573.

www.ingramcontent.com/pod-product-compliance
Lightning Source LLC
Chambersburg PA
CBHW062208080426
42734CB00010B/1836